THE WEAKEST LINK
QUIZ BOOK

THE WEAKEST LINK
QUIZ BOOK

PENGUIN BOOKS

Published by the Penguin Group
Penguin Books Ltd, 27 Wrights Lane, London W8 5TZ, England
Penguin Putnam Inc., 375 Hudson Street, New York, New York 10014, USA
Penguin Books Australia Ltd, Ringwood, Victoria, Australia
Penguin Books Canada Ltd, 10 Alcorn Avenue, Toronto, Ontario, Canada M4V
3B2
Penguin Books India (P) Ltd, 11 Community Centre, Panchsheel Park,
New Delhi - 110 017, India
Penguin Books (NZ) Ltd, Cnr Rosedale and Airborne Roads,
Albany, Auckland, New Zealand
Penguin Books (South Africa) (Pty) Ltd, 5 Watkins Street, Denver Ext 4,
Johannesburg 2094, South Africa
Penguin Books Ltd, Registered Offices: Harmondsworth, Middlesex, England

First published 2001
1 3 5 7 9 10 8 6 4 2

Set in Futura Light
Printed in England by Clays Ltd, St Ives plc

CONTENTS

HOW TO PLAY

THE RULES

Weakest Link is a quiz game with a difference – in order to win, the players must act as a team, working together to build chains of correct answers and eliminating the players who are the weakest links and most often break the chain. To become the final champion you'll need to use both your general knowledge and your strategic skills: should you 'bank' the points in the chain or risk losing them all by failing to answer your question correctly? Can you spot who is the weakest link in the team? Should you vote them out, or try to eliminate the team-mate who may be your biggest threat when it comes to the final round? Or will you be taking the 'walk of shame' as you are voted the weakest link?

Now you can experience the excitement, tension and perhaps even embarrassment of the TV quiz show by playing the game at home, with *The Weakest Link Quiz Book*. Here's how to play:

What You Need

Weakest Link can be played by any number of players but ideally there should be four or more, one of whom will be the quiz master (see page 9 for how to play with two or three players or on your own).

Each player will need a pencil and a sheet or pad of paper. The quiz master may also want a pencil and paper to keep a tally of the scores. If you want to give each round a time limit, you will need a watch with a second hand or a stopwatch.

The Rounds

The quiz master takes the book and opens it to the Questions section. At the beginning of the first round the quiz master asks the first question to the player whose initial is the earliest in the alphabet, the second question to the player on his or her left, and so on, asking each player a question in turn. In the following rounds the person to the left of the last player to answer a question in the previous round is the first to be asked.

The length of each round can be determined in a number of ways:

Timing: As in *The Weakest Link* TV programme, each round can have a time limit, starting with 3 minutes for the first round, and cutting off 10 seconds with each further round. Round two would therefore be 2 minutes 50 seconds, round three 2 minutes 40 seconds, round four 2 minutes 30 seconds, and so on. In this case you may use up the questions of more than two pages in each round. In the first round the quiz master will have to keep watch on the time; in later rounds one of the players who has been eliminated could be responsible for the timing.

20 Questions: You could limit each round to 20 questions (two pages of the book).

Questions Per Player: Alternatively you could decide to ask each player three, four or five questions in each round. Again, the quiz master might use up the questions on more than two pages and would have to carry the scoring over.

Scoring

The quiz master is responsible for keeping a tally of the team's score for each round, using the points chain on each right-hand page. At the beginning of the round, he or she puts a finger, or the point of a pencil, on the bottom link of the chain, the zero. If the question is answered correctly, the quiz master will move his or her finger or pencil up to the next link – 20. If the second question is answered correctly he or she moves it up to the third link – 50, and so on. If the player gets the answer wrong, the chain is broken and must start again at zero.

The aim of the players is to work as a team to collect as many points as possible during the round. To do this they must bank the points before the chain is broken by a wrong answer or the round comes to an end. They do this by calling 'bank' when it comes to their turn to answer a question, but before the question has been asked. When 'bank' is called, the quiz master writes down the score reached at that point either in the spaces below the points chain on the page or on a separate piece of paper. The quiz master then puts his or her finger or pencil back on zero to start a new chain and asks the player who has banked the points his or her question.

It is up to the skill and judgement of each player whether to bank the points, thereby securing the points but breaking the chain, or to carry on and try to build the chain higher, but risk losing it all if they can't answer the question correctly.

At the end of the game, only points that have been banked count. If the last player to be questioned does not call 'bank' before his or her question, the points on the current chain are lost. The players cannot see the chain, but to help them keep track of how the points are building, the quiz master should call out 'zero' at the beginning of each chain (that is, whenever a question is answered incorrectly, or the points are banked).

At the end of the first round the quiz master adds up all the points banked. This balance is then brought forward to the next round, and can be written in the space at the top of the next right-hand page to keep a running total of the points for the game.

The Weakest Link

At the end of each round, each player must decide who has been the weakest link, answering the fewest questions correctly or failing to bank points. The players write their selection on their pieces of paper, which they hold up at the same time. The player with the most votes is the weakest link and must leave the game.

In the event of a draw, responsibility for naming the weakest link lies with those who have already been voted off as weakest links. These players should continue to keep track of the game so that they can cast their votes if necessary. And maybe settle some old scores!

Once the weakest link has been decided, the quiz master starts a new round with the remaining players.

The Last Round

When there are only two players left, they have the opportunity to increase the points by playing an extra round after which the total points for that round are trebled before being added to the running total. It is these points that the two players will then play for in the Final.

The Final

After the last round the two remaining players go head-to-head in a final battle to find out who is the strongest link. The players take it in turns to answer ten questions each. These questions can be found in the Finals section at the back of the book. The quiz master can mark each question with a tick if it is answered correctly, or a cross if it is answered incorrectly, in the spaces provided. The player who was the strongest link in the previous round (as decided by either the quiz

master or the players no longer in the game) can decide whether to
answer first or second.

The player who answers the most questions correctly is the winner,
and the strongest link. If there is a tie after ten questions, the players
will each be asked a tie-break question from the last pages of the
book. If both players answer their questions correctly, another two
questions are asked, and so on until one player fails to answer their
question while the other player gets theirs right.

Playing with Two or Three Players

You can use *The Weakest Link Quiz Book* to test the general
knowledge and skill of two or three players. In this case, players
should take it in turns to ask a round of questions to one opponent.
After each question the player has the chance to bank his or her
points or continue and try to build up the chain of points.

After 20 questions, or if you wish to time the rounds three minutes,
the round ends and the player's points are counted. That player then
becomes the quiz master for the next round. If there are three players,
he will question the third player, who will then test the first quiz master
in the next round. If there are two players they simply take it in turns to
be quiz master. After a set number of rounds, decided before the
beginning of the game, the player with the most points is the winner.

Testing Your Own Knowledge

Of course, you can also use *The Weakest Link Quiz Book* on your
own to test your general knowledge. Try to answer 20 questions, then
check to see how many you got right. Cover up the answers until the
end of the round! Allocate yourself one point for each question
answered correctly and see if you can improve your score with the
next round.

1 The Burmese is a variety of which household animal?

2 The song 'It Ain't Necessarily So' comes from which opera by George Gershwin?

3 Of which style of architecture is Burghley House near Stamford an example, Elizabethan or Victorian?

4 Jay Kaye, from the band Jamiroquai, is the partner of which television presenter?

5 In which century did Alfred Lord Tennyson become the English Poet Laureate?

6 The oil terminal of Sullom Voe is in which island group, the Shetlands or the Outer Hebrides?

7 Who succeeded Fulgencio Batista as the leader of Cuba in 1959?

8 Which English playwright is famous for his *Talking Heads* series?

9 Which Australian television entertainer had a hit in 1960 with 'Tie me Kangaroo Down, Sport'?

10 In which decade of the twentieth century was the first American football Super Bowl held?

11 Which World War II British twin-engined aircraft, mostly built of wood, shared its name with an insect?

12 Which actor stars in the western film *The Outlaw Josey Wales*?

13 In human biology, the scapula and patella are both types of what?

14 What geographical feature, beginning with *T*, is a river that flows into another river, rather than into a lake or the sea?

15 Is the scientific symbol of the male a circle with an arrow or a circle with a cross?

16 In fashion, what are moccasins?

17 In which decade of the twentieth century was the Duke of Edinburgh's Award Scheme launched?

18 The Royal Northern College of Music is based in which city?

19 With which sport would you associate Brendan Foster?

20 In America, the Gettysburg Address was made during which war?

Answers

1 Cat
2 *Porgy and Bess*
3 Elizabethan
4 Denise van Outen
5 Nineteenth century (1850)
6 Shetlands
7 Fidel (Ruz) Castro (accept Fidel Castro Ruz or just Castro)
8 Alan Bennett
9 Rolf Harris
10 1960s
11 Mosquito (accept De Havilland DH-98 Mosquito)

12 Clint Eastwood
13 Bone
14 Tributary
15 Arrow
16 Shoes (accept slippers)
17 1950s (1956)
18 Manchester
19 Athletics (accept running or middle-/long-distance running; also accept 1500 m, 3000 m, 5000 m, 10,000 m and 2 miles)
20 American Civil War (accept the war between the states)

1 Which breed of cattle, originating in Scotland, is distinguished by its long shaggy coats and large curved horns?

2 What is the national airline of Germany?

3 Who is president of the National Society for the Prevention of Cruelty to Children?

4 In pop music, Claire, Lee, Faye, H and Lisa are the members of which chart-topping band?

5 The pilgrims in Chaucer's *Canterbury Tales* were travelling to Canterbury from where?

6 In which decade of the twentieth century did Yasser Arafat become chairman of the Palestine Liberation Organisation?

7 Which actor battles aliens in the films *Independence Day* and *Men In Black*?

8 The mountain range called the Southern Alps is in which country?

9 In food, nan and soda are both types of what?

10 Which pop singer had a hit in 1961 with 'Hit the Road Jack'?

11 In human biology, are 'venules' the smallest or largest veins?

12 What relation was Miss Ellie to JR in the American television soap *Dallas*?

13 In science, how many degrees Kelvin is absolute zero?

14 Of which country was Ehud Barak elected prime minister in May 1999?

15 In maths, what A is the highest point of a solid relative to its base?

16 In the animal kingdom, the hippopotamus is indigenous to which continent?

17 In Scotland, who was the first person to become 'Lady of the Thistle'?

18 What are the first two letters in the Belfast postcode?

19 In which sport are the terms 'divot' and 'apron' used?

20 In English literature, whose sonnets are written to a mysterious 'Dark Lady'?

Previous Total

1,000
800
600
450
300
200
100
50
20
0

Banked

Total

Answers

1 Highland
2 Lufthansa
3 Princess Margaret (accept [HRH] Princess Margaret [Rose], or Countess of Snowdon)
4 Steps
5 London (accept The Tabard Inn, Southwark)
6 1960s
7 Will Smith
8 New Zealand (South Island)
9 Bread
10 Ray Charles

11 Smallest veins
12 His mother
13 Zero
14 Israel
15 Apex
16 Africa
17 [HM Queen Elizabeth] The Queen Mother
18 BT
19 Golf
20 [William] Shakespeare's

Round 3

1 In geography, Abuja is the capital of which African nation?

2 Which British television comedy quiz show featured the 'dove from above'?

3 From which English county does Purbeck marble come?

4 In food, which meat is traditionally used for the Italian dish 'ossobuco'?

5 Which member of the Bach family wrote the Brandenburg Concertos, Johann Christian or Johann Sebastian?

6 Which of these is a tool: a hassock, a mattock or a hummock?

7 In which game would you play with a 'double-six' and 'double-blank'?

8 In the army, how many stripes or chevrons are there on a sergeant's badge of rank?

9 In literature, what was the first name of the poet C. Day Lewis?

10 In the animal kingdom, by what one-word name is the American prairie wolf also known?

11 Which television cartoon series features the characters Ned Flanders and Mr Burns?

12 In which decade of the nineteenth century was Euston, London's first mainline station, opened?

13 In astrology, in which two months could you have been born if your star sign is Aquarius?

14 Which American jazz singer was called the 'First Lady of Song'?

15 The flesh of which animal does a hippophagist eat?

16 Which of London's airports lies just off junction 8 of the M11 motorway?

17 Who played the policeman trying to stop Wesley Snipes in the 1993 film *Demolition Man*?

18 In which county is the village of Aldermaston?

19 The delphinium flower gets its name from its supposed resemblance to which sea creature?

20 In science, what term describes dissimilar organisms living together in a mutually beneficial relationship?

Previous Total

( )

(1,000)

(800)

(600)

(450)

(300)

(200)

(100)

(50)

(20)

(0)

Banked

( )
( )
( )
( )
( )

Total

( )

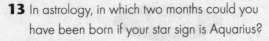

Answers

1 Nigeria	**11** *The Simpsons*
2 *Shooting Stars*	**12** 1830s (1837)
3 Dorset	**13** January and February
4 Veal	**14** Ella Fitzgerald
5 Johann Sebastian	**15** Horse
6 Mattock	**16** Stansted
7 Dominoes	**17** Sylvester Stallone
8 Three	**18** [West] Berkshire
9 Cecil	**19** Dolphin
10 Coyote	**20** Symbiosis

Round 4

1 In the human body, gingiva is tissue from which part of the mouth?

2 Where would a Scotsman wear his tam-o'-shanter?

3 Which American computer company developed the first word processor in 1965?

4 Which company opened Britain's first large scale car factory in Coventry in 1896?

5 What was the name of the boy who climbed the giant beanstalk in the folk tale?

6 In which English county is the beach called 'Sands'?

7 In pop music, which former member of Take That had a monster hit with the song 'Angels'?

8 In the television series, Reginald Perrin's boss was known by which two letters?

9 Which director's films include *Beetlejuice*, *Batman* and *Sleepy Hollow*?

10 A licence for what form of entertainment cost 10 shillings when it was introduced in 1927?

11 General Galtieri resigned as the president of which country in June 1982 in the wake of the Falklands conflict?

12 Which country does golf legend Seve Ballesteros come from?

13 In geography, 'crest' and 'breaker' are both terms used to describe what?

14 In Britain, how many days after Hallowe'en is Bonfire Night?

15 The Church of Scientology was founded in which country?

16 The seeds of which plant, with the botanical name *Papaver somniferum*, are used to top bread and rolls?

17 In food, minestrone soup originates from which country?

18 In astrology, which sign of the zodiac is symbolised by two fish?

19 Which unpopular tax was introduced in Scotland in 1989 and into England and Wales the following year?

20 Who played Mrs Slocombe in the television series *Are You Being Served*?

Previous Total

1,000

800

600

450

300

200

100

50

20

0

Banked

Total

Answers

1 Gums
2 On his head
3 IBM
4 Daimler
5 Jack
6 North Yorkshire (accept Yorkshire but make clear it is North Yorkshire specifically)
7 Robbie Williams
8 C. J.
9 Tim Burton
10 Radio
11 Argentina
12 Spain
13 Waves (the sea)
14 5 days
15 America (accept USA)
16 (Opium) poppy
17 Italy
18 Pisces
19 Community Charge (accept poll tax)
20 Molly Sugden

Round 5

1 Which nineteenth-century author wrote the novel *Dombey and Son*?

2 Who was replaced as German chancellor in 1998, after sixteen years in power?

3 Which television guide was 75 years old in 1998?

4 Which cereal crop is also known in the United States as Indian corn?

5 Which garden flower, a favourite of Dame Edna Everage, is sometimes known as the sword lily?

6 What is the highest denomination postal order that can be bought?

7 In television, who starred as Mr Gordon Brittas in *The Brittas Empire*?

8 Which surrealist artist created the Lobster Telephone, owned by the Tate Gallery?

9 Which workers' organisations were banned by the Combination Acts of 1799 and 1800?

10 Which American author, known for his horror stories, wrote the poem 'The Raven' in 1845?

11 Who played the male and female leads in the film *Grease*?

12 In design, what does the acronym CAD stand for?

13 Who recorded the 1980s song 'Like a Prayer' that had its video condemned by the Vatican?

14 Which surgical instrument, similar to tongs, is used to aid childbirth?

15 In the fairy tale *Cinderella*, what vegetable turns into the carriage?

16 Which American president famously said, 'The ballot is stronger than the bullet'?

17 In television, Eliot Ness was the federal agent at the centre of which US crime show?

18 Which actress played the Marilyn Monroe role in *The Seven Year Itch* in the West End from October 2000?

19 Which German composer wrote the cycle of four operas *The Ring of the Nibelung*?

20 What is the nationality of world champion gymnast Svetlana Khorkina?

Previous Total

1,000

800

600

450

300

200

100

50

20

0

Banked

Total

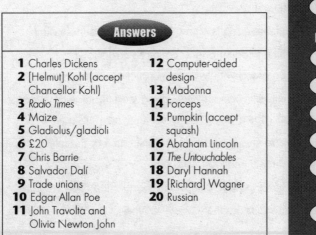

Answers

1 Charles Dickens
2 [Helmut] Kohl (accept Chancellor Kohl)
3 *Radio Times*
4 Maize
5 Gladiolus/gladioli
6 £20
7 Chris Barrie
8 Salvador Dalí
9 Trade unions
10 Edgar Allan Poe
11 John Travolta and Olivia Newton John
12 Computer-aided design
13 Madonna
14 Forceps
15 Pumpkin (accept squash)
16 Abraham Lincoln
17 *The Untouchables*
18 Daryl Hannah
19 [Richard] Wagner
20 Russian

Round 6

1 In which country are Rotterdam and Eindhoven?

2 In the children's television series *Sooty*, what is the name of his dog friend?

3 In maths, 39.37 inches are equivalent to how many metres?

4 What is the first name of the founder of the Williams Formula One motor racing team?

5 In which of the arts was Barbara Hepworth one of the most influential figures of the mid-twentieth century?

6 SEN and SRN were formerly initials indicating a level of training in which profession?

7 Sony Music president Tommy Mottola was married to which vocalist?

8 Roughly two miles long, what is the name of Venice's main canal?

9 If a female pig is a sow, what you call a male pig?

10 Which Mediterranean country's flag shows a gold map of an island with two olive branches underneath?

11 Family allowances were introduced in Britain in 1946 at 5 shillings a week. What are they now called?

12 In pop music, what was the first name of the late American musician Zappa?

13 What is the last letter of the Greek alphabet?

14 Bracken is a variety of which type of plant?

15 In the human body, what is the medical name for the collarbone?

16 In food, what type of dish is bortsch?

17 What were the names of the self-sufficient couple whose neighbours were Margot and Jerry in the sitcom *The Good Life*?

18 The Adi Granth is the holy book of which religion?

19 How many times did cyclist Miguel Indurain win the Tour de France in the 1990s?

20 Which 1971 children's film featured Angela Lansbury as a student of witchcraft?

Previous Total

1,000

800

600

450

300

200

100

50

20

0

Banked

Total

Answers

1 The Netherlands/ Holland
2 Sweep
3 One
4 Francis (accept Frank)
5 Sculpture
6 Nurse/nursing (accept medicine, medical)
7 Mariah Carey
8 Grand Canal (accept Canale Grande)
9 Boar
10 Cyprus

11 Child Benefit
12 Frank (accept Francis)
13 Omega
14 Fern
15 Clavicle
16 Soup (accept stew)
17 Barbara and Tom (surname Good)
18 Sikhism
19 Five
20 *Bedknobs and Broomsticks*

1 In language, what term is used to describe a word sounding like the thing it refers to?

2 Who originally played the role taken by Rene Russo in the remake of *The Thomas Crown Affair*?

3 In which game might you play with an 'alley' and a 'taw'?

4 Sir Thomas More wrote a history of which English king that has caused people ever since to regard him as a murderous villain?

5 By which three initials is an electrocardiograph commonly known?

6 Which female pop singer had hits with 'Luka' and 'Marlene on the Wall'?

7 San Juan is the capital of which island in the West Indies?

8 What style of architecture developed in England and Normandy between the eleventh and twelfth centuries?

9 Who wrote the autobiography *The Naked Civil Servant*?

10 In England, OFSTED is the Office for Standards in what field?

11 Nelli Kim was an Olympic star in which sport?

12 Which English economist published *The General Theory of Employment Interest and Money* in 1936?

13 The grub of the crane fly, a common garden pest, is commonly known as what *L*?

14 In the human body, are 'carpals' bones that make up the wrist or ankle joint?

15 Which City of London landmark boasts a high dome and is 365 feet from ground level to its highest point?

16 What is the specific non-slang term for a native of Liverpool?

17 Which of these African countries is further north, Zambia or Libya?

18 Complete the title of this 1995 film starring Sean Penn: *Dead Man . . .* what?

19 In America, what letter is used to classify that a film is suitable for all?

20 In 1818, who wrote the novel *Frankenstein*?

Previous Total

1,000

800

600

450

300

200

100

50

20

0

Banked

Total

Answers

1 Onomatopoeia
2 Faye Dunaway
3 Marbles
4 Richard III (accept Richard Crookback)
5 ECG
6 Suzanne Vega
7 Puerto Rico
8 Norman/Romanesque
9 Quentin Crisp
10 Education (accept schools or teaching)
11 Gymnastics
12 [John Maynard] Keynes (accept J. M. Keynes)
13 Leatherjacket
14 Wrist
15 St Paul's Cathedral
16 Liverpudlian
17 Libya
18 *Walking*
19 G
20 Mary Shelley (accept Mary [Wollstonecraft] Shelley/Mary [Wollstonecraft] Godwin)

Round 8

1 The Dutch lens grinder Hans Lippershey is credited with making the first of which type of optical instrument?

2 With which ancient empire is the toga most associated?

3 How many Indiana Jones movies, directed by Steven Spielberg, have there been?

4 In sport, on what would you find a 'doubles ring' and a 'trebles ring'?

5 Which government agency is responsible for registering and licensing motor vehicles in Britain?

6 In the television series, did David Soul play Starsky or Hutch?

7 In literature, complete the title of the Frederick Forsyth novel: *The Fourth . . .*

8 In physics, what *V* is another word for capacity?

9 In the animal kingdom, is the dugong a land animal or marine animal?

10 When telephoning abroad from a UK land line, what are the first two digits dialled?

11 In English law, the act of criminally setting fire to property is known as what?

12 The Celine Dion song 'My Heart Will Go On' comes from which film?

13 In ancient history, the gods Horus, Apis and Hathor were from which country?

14 In America, MA is the abbreviation for which state?

15 Which of these airports is furthest from London by plane, Dublin or Shannon?

16 In which 1984 film was the line 'I'll be back' delivered by Arnold Schwarzenegger?

17 In food, is the leek an allium or a brassica?

18 In nature, which plant is the principal diet of the caterpillar of the Red Admiral butterfly?

19 In pop music, which large, accident-prone, spotted character had a Christmas number one in 1993?

20 What was the maiden name of the bride whose royal wedding took place on 19 June 1999 in St George's Chapel, Windsor?

Previous Total

1,000
800
600
450
300
200
100
50
20
0

Banked

Total

Answers

1 (Refracting) telescope
2 Roman
3 Three
4 Dartboard
5 DVLA, the Driver and Vehicle Licensing Agency (do *not* accept DVLC)
6 Hutch
7 *Protocol*
8 Volume
9 Marine
10 OO
11 Arson
12 *Titanic*
13 Egypt
14 Massachusetts
15 Shannon
16 *The Terminator*
17 An allium
18 (Stinging) nettle
19 Mr Blobby
20 Sophie Rhys-Jones (to Prince Edward)

Round 9

1 What name is given to the US president's office in the White House because of its shape?

2 In 1946, honeymooner Maisie Dunn was said to be the first person in Britain to wear which item of beachwear?

3 In maths, if 10 pesetas equals 5 pence, how much does 30 pesetas equal?

4 Is it true or false that the supersaurus and the ultrasaurus were among the world's largest dinosaurs?

5 Which annual international competition has been won by Abba, Bucks Fizz, and Lulu?

6 Ankara is the capital city of which country?

7 In the USA, which government organisation has the initials DEA?

8 Which *T* is a type of dog whose name is derived from the Latin word for 'ground'?

9 Karl Dahlman was inspired by the hovercraft to invent which aid to gardeners?

10 Which comedy duo's appreciation society is called Sons of the Desert, from the title of one of their early films?

11 In the human body, is the epidermis beneath or above the dermis?

12 By what name is the Palace of Westminster also known?

13 Which television sitcom starred Karl Howman as a womanizing painter and decorator?

14 A campanile is a tower which normally houses what?

15 What is the name of the bear who is used to promote the BBC's annual Children in Need appeal?

16 In food, which R is a dish originating from France, primarily made from aubergines and green peppers in a tomato sauce?

17 In the royal family, who is the father of Lord Frederick and Lady Gabriella Windsor?

18 In pop music, the British band Manic Street Preachers are from which country?

19 In English history, who defeated Harold II at the Battle of Hastings?

20 In literature, who wrote the series of Adrian Mole diaries?

Previous Total

1,000
800
600
450
300
200
100
50
20
0

Banked

Total

Answers

1 The Oval Office
2 Bikini (accept two-piece swimsuit)
3 15 pence
4 True
5 Eurovision Song Contest
6 Turkey
7 Drug Enforcement Agency
8 Terrier
9 Hover mower/Flymo
10 [Stan] Laurel and [Oliver] Hardy
11 Beneath
12 The Houses of Parliament (do not accept House of Commons or Lords)
13 *Brush Strokes*
14 Bells
15 Pudsey
16 Ratatouille
17 Prince Michael [of Kent]
18 Wales (do not accept Britain)
19 William the Conqueror (accept William of Normandy/William I of England/William II of Normandy/William the Bastard)
20 Sue Townsend

Round 10

1 With what sport would you primarily associate the promoter Don King?

2 In the human body, what S is the uncontrolled contraction of a muscle or group of muscles?

3 Which screen siren played the character Sugar Kane in the film Some Like It Hot?

4 A museum dedicated to which fabled local resident can be found at Drumnadrochit in the Scottish Highlands?

5 In herbal medicine, which wort is said to be a cure for depression?

6 In languages, what is the usual French word for butter?

7 In geography, the Namib Desert is in which continent?

8 In television, which presenter's catchphrase is 'Hello, good evening and welcome'?

9 In pop music, the Queen song 'We Will Rock You' was re-released by which boy band in 2000?

10 With which sport would you associate Rob Andrew?

11 The American Earl Tupper is credited with inventing which method of storage?

12 In history, Claus von Stauffenberg led a plot to assassinate which German in 1944?

13 In medicine, what part of the body is operated on during root-canal surgery?

14 What nationality is the famous fashion designer Valentino?

15 In literature, which series of novels about a family was written by John Galsworthy?

16 In folklore, which Y is another name for the Abominable Snowman?

17 In which county is the coastal resort of Aldeburgh?

18 Which 1970s American pop group had members who dressed as a construction worker, a policeman, a soldier and a cowboy?

19 In the UK, which material is traditionally associated with the fifth wedding anniversary?

20 Who played Captain Billy Tyne in the year 2000 film *The Perfect Storm*?

Previous Total

1,000
800
600
450
300
200
100
50
20
0

Banked

Total

Answers

1 Boxing
2 Spasm (accept spastic contraction, *do not* accept shake)
3 Marilyn Monroe
4 Loch Ness monster
5 St John's Wort
6 Beurre
7 Africa
8 David Frost
9 Five
10 Rugby union (accept rugby)
11 Tupperware (accept airtight plastic storage container)
12 Adolf Hitler (accept the [or Der] Führer and Schicklgrüber)
13 Teeth (accept gums or mouth)
14 Italian
15 The *Forsyte Saga*
16 Yeti
17 Suffolk
18 Village People
19 Wood
20 George Clooney

Round 11

1 In the American military, what does the *A* stand for in KIA?

2 In transport, what were first installed on 21 dangerous roads in west London in October 1992?

3 In food, what is the name given to the small Italian dumplings that can be served in place of pasta?

4 In football, what is the principal colour of Leeds United's home strip?

5 Which ancient Greek wrote, in his classic text named *Politics*, that 'man is by nature a political animal'?

6 In nature, which birch tree gets its name from the distinctive colour of its bark?

7 In UK business, what is the tax on company profits called?

8 In television, David Yip played which detective in the 1980s show of the same name?

9 In geography, Abu Simbel is the site of two ancient temples on the banks of which river?

10 What is the usual name for the animal and its fur also known as cony?

11 Which actress was the recipient of Dudley Moore's attention in the film *10*?

12 Felipe Gonzalez was prime minister of which European country from 1982 to 1996?

13 Which *K* is the winged seed of the ash and several other trees?

14 In which American city was the television comedy *Cheers* set?

15 Which Ancient Greek philosopher wrote the philosophical dialogue the *Phaedo*?

16 Who won the Best Supporting Actress award at the year 2000 Oscar ceremony for her role in the film *Girl, Interrupted*?

17 In the human body, what is the lymph tissue at the back of the nose more commonly called?

18 In the television programme *The Muppet Show*, who was in love with Kermit the Frog?

19 Lake Eyre is found in which country?

20 Which German city, firebombed in 1945, is associated with fine porcelain?

Previous Total

1,000

800

600

450

300

200

100

50

20

0

Banked

Total

Answers

1 Action	**10** Rabbit
2 Speed cameras	**11** Bo Derek
3 Gnocchi	**12** Spain
4 White	**13** Key(s)
5 Aristotle	**14** Boston
6 Silver birch	**15** Plato
7 Corporation tax	**16** Angelina Jolie
(accept corporate	**17** Adenoids
income tax)	**18** Miss Piggy
8 *The Chinese Detective*	**19** Australia
9 The Nile	**20** Dresden

Round 12

1 Which David is an English artist famed for his paintings of Californian swimming pools?

2 In law, taking legal steps to reduce your tax bill is called tax avoidance. What is taking illegal steps called?

3 Who sang the Bond theme tune 'Goldeneye'?

4 In medicine, what do the initials IVF stand for?

5 In which modern country is Thessaloniki?

6 Which county is the chief setting for Winston Graham's *Poldark* novels?

7 King Charles XVI Gustaf is monarch of which European country?

8 What is the name of the volcano which erupted in Washington State on 18 May 1980?

9 Which sport or pastime consists of propelling yourself on skates resembling ice skates but fitted with wheels?

10 In opera, what was the first name of the twentieth-century tenor Caruso?

11 Which disease, carried by mosquitoes and mainly associated with hotter climates, was known as ague in Elizabethan times?

12 What is the name of the chief executive of the Millennium Dome who was replaced in February 2000?

13 Which painter abandoned his life as a Parisian stockbroker to become an artist?

14 What kind of creature is a marlin?

15 Which canal links the Red Sea and the Mediterranean?

16 Which Lloyd Webber musical contains the song 'Love Changes Everything'?

17 In nature, which garden plant is named after the Swedish botanist Anders Dahl?

18 Who invented the system, which bears his name, for reducing the hiss on audio tapes?

19 In food, what is the name of the Spanish chilled soup containing tomatoes and garlic?

20 In the animal kingdom, the 'Suffolk punch' is a variety of what?

Previous Total

1,000

800

600

450

300

200

100

50

20

0

Banked

Total

Answers

1 David Hockney
2 Tax evasion
3 Tina Turner
4 *In vitro* fertilisation
5 Greece (do not accept Macedonia)
6 Cornwall
7 Sweden
8 Mount St Helen's
9 Rollerblading (accept in-line skating or rollerskating)
10 Enrico
11 Malaria
12 Jennie Page (accept Jennifer Page)
13 Paul Gauguin
14 Fish (accept swordfish)
15 The Suez Canal
16 *Aspects of Love*
17 Dahlia
18 [Ray] Dolby
19 Gazpacho
20 [Shire] horse

Round 13

1 In the nursery rhyme 'Ring a ring o' roses', what is a pocket full of?

2 Which author wrote the novels *A Widow for One Year* and *A Prayer for Owen Meany*?

3 Which punk band was the subject of the film *The Filth and the Fury*?

4 In maths, if a box of nails weighs 2000 grams, how many kilograms does it weigh?

5 The 'Ode to Joy' from Beethoven's Choral symphony is the anthem of which European political body?

6 Who played Ripley in the *Alien* series of films?

7 In computer languages, what is 'beginner's all-purpose symbolic instruction code' better known as?

8 On whose books were the films *Howard's End* and *A Room With a View* based?

9 In dressmaking, which *D* describes a stitched fold of material tapered to a narrow point?

10 With which sport would you associate the Portuguese sportsman Eusebio?

11 In medicine, which *I* is a respirator consisting of an airtight metal chamber encasing the body?

12 What is the French name for the mountain the Italians call Monte Bianco?

13 In pop music, Richard Ashcroft was the former lead singer with which group?

14 In which European country is the resort of Antibes?

15 Who played the lead character, Alex, in Stanley Kubrick's film version of *A Clockwork Orange*?

16 For which religious leader was Terry Waite acting as special envoy at the time of his kidnapping in Beirut in 1987?

17 Which English architect designed Castle Howard and Blenheim Palace?

18 In carpentry, 'countersunk', 'raised head' and 'round head' are types of what?

19 Which book by Richard Adams features the characters Hazel, Fiver and Bigwig?

20 Which castle is the present official home of the Anglican Bishop of Durham?

Previous Total
( )
1,000
800
600
450
300
200
100
50
20
0
Banked
( )
( )
( )
( )
( )
( )
Total
( )

Answers

1 Posies
2 John Irving
3 The Sex Pistols
4 Two kilograms
5 European Union
6 Sigourney Weaver
7 BASIC
8 E. M. Forster (Edward Morgan Foster)
9 Dart
10 Football (accept soccer)
11 Iron lung (*do not* accept incubator)
12 Mont Blanc
13 The Verve
14 France
15 Malcolm McDowell
16 Archbishop of Canterbury (Dr Robert Runcie)
17 [Sir John] Vanbrugh
18 Screws
19 *Watership Down*
20 Auckland Castle

Round 14

1 The island of Zealand is part of which European country?

2 Is the 'pleura' part of the human body or part of a plant?

3 In chess, which piece can legally move only diagonally?

4 In the animal kingdom, are polar bears native to the Arctic or the Antarctic?

5 In furniture, what is a Chesterfield?

6 Which cartoon character is famous for eating spinach?

7 Did Albert Einstein announce his Special Theory of Relativity in the year 1895 or 1905?

8 In nature, which Y is an evergreen tree widely associated with immortality and life after death?

9 Which sport did Mike Gatting play for England?

10 Which book did Charles Darwin publish in 1859 to explain his theory of evolution?

11 In architecture, were Robert and James Adam eighteenth-century masters of the neoclassical style or the medieval style?

12 In Judaism, what is the Hebrew word for 'proper'?

13 In dentistry, what name is given to the thin, fibrous material inserted between teeth to remove food and plaque?

14 Which Italian city is home to statues of David by Donatello and Michelangelo?

15 On an Ordnance Survey map, what does 'MS' stand for?

16 What is James Bond's favourite drink?

17 In the animal kingdom, are Jersey cattle dairy or beef cattle?

18 In the UK, what is the telephone dialling code for Belfast?

19 What gas is added to soft drinks to make them fizzy?

20 Which UK political party's headquarters are at the Dog and Partridge pub in Yateley, Hampshire?

Previous Total

1,000

800

600

450

300

200

100

50

20

0

Banked

Total

Answers

1 Denmark
2 Human body
3 Bishop
4 Arctic
5 Couch/sofa/settee/ divan
6 Popeye
7 1905
8 Yew
9 Cricket
10 [On] *The Origin of Species*
11 Neoclassical
12 Kosher

13 Dental floss (accept floss/dental tape)
14 Florence
15 Milestone
16 Vodka martini (shaken, not stirred) (accept vodka martini or just martini)
17 Dairy
18 02890
19 Carbon dioxide
20 Monster Raving Loony Party

1 Which of Queen Elizabeth the Queen Mother's relatives succeeded her as chancellor of London University?

2 In the UK, from the year 2000, what are the first two digits of all new mobile phone numbers?

3 In maths, which semicircular plastic instrument is used for measuring angles?

4 Which dictator, executed by partisans in 1945, was known as 'Il Duce'?

5 In a US postal address, ND is the abbreviation for which state?

6 In which century did William Wordsworth become the English Poet Laureate?

7 In fashion, what is a parka?

8 Which film featuring 'Kermit and his friends' is based on a Dickens novel?

9 Which of these cities is furthest from London by plane: Harare or Havana?

10 In food, is chervil a spice or a herb?

11 In pop music, 'We Are The Champions' was a hit in 1977 for which group?

12 In which century did Lord Lovat become the last person in England to be judicially executed by beheading?

13 The EPCOT Center is a tourist attraction in which American state?

14 A variety of which cereal plant produces corn on the cob or sweetcorn?

15 Is the 'Casparian strip' part of Greece or part of a plant?

16 What Q is another name for the chemical element mercury?

17 In television, 'That's Living All Right' was the theme tune to which comedy drama of the 1980s?

18 In which year of the twentieth century was Germany officially reunited?

19 In history, was 'bull-leaping' a popular sport in Crete or Majorca?

20 In the UK, what are the first two letters in the Chelmsford postcode?

Previous Total

1,000

800

600

450

300

200

100

50

20

0

Banked

Total

Answers

1 [HRH] The Princess Royal (accept Princess Anne)
2 07
3 Protractor
4 Mussolini (accept Benito Mussolini/ Amilcare Andrea)
5 North Dakota
6 Nineteenth century (actually: 1843)
7 Overcoat/jacket/coat (accept anorak)
8 *The Muppet Christmas Carol*
9 Harare
10 Herb
11 Queen
12 Eighteenth century
13 Florida
14 Maize
15 Part of a plant (in the walls of the endodermis)
16 Quicksilver
17 *Auf Wiedersehen, Pet*
18 1990
19 Crete
20 CM

Round 16

1 With what sport would you associate Australian Greg Norman?

2 In which country was the novelist and playwright Samuel Beckett born?

3 In the Bible, did God tell Noah to build the ark out of cypress wood or pine wood?

4 What is the British word for the part of a railway that Americans call 'switches'?

5 In botany, what *P* is the stalk of a leaf called?

6 Which famous painting by Leonardo da Vinci did Francis I of France buy for his bathroom?

7 Blanche Dubois and Stanley Kowalski appear in which Tennessee Williams play?

8 In education, Homerton College of Education is part of which British university?

9 In the doh, ray, me musical scale, which note proceeds soh?

10 Which fruit has varieties called Granny Smith, Golden Delicious and Gala?

11 Which British city is the home of the Royal Liver Building?

12 Which BBC radio station was the first to broadcast nationally 24 hours a day?

13 In which decade was National Service abolished in the UK?

14 In business, do Public Limited Companies or Private Limited Companies sell their shares on the stock market?

15 In the animal kingdom, the extinct bird the moa was native to which country, Australia or New Zealand?

16 Which former Wimbledon footballer appeared in the year 2000 film *Snatch*?

17 What part of the body is odontophobia a fear of?

18 In 1930, who became the first woman to fly solo from Britain to Australia?

19 Babbacombe Bay, Slapton Sands and Ilfracombe are all beaches in which English county?

20 In gardening, 'Mrs Popple' is a variety of which flower?

Previous Total

1,000
800
600
450
300
200
100
50
20
0

Banked

Total

Answers

1 Golf	**10** Apple
2 Ireland (accept Eire, Southern Ireland, Republic of Ireland)	**11** Liverpool
	12 Radio 2
	13 1960s
3 Cypress wood	**14** Public Limited Companies
4 Points	
5 Petiole	**15** New Zealand
6 The *Mona Lisa*	**16** Vinnie Jones
7 *A Streetcar Named Desire*	**17** Teeth
	18 Amy Johnson
8 Cambridge	**19** Devon
9 Fah	**20** Fuchsia

Round 17

1 Which Hollywood actor had a pop hit with the song 'Gettin' Jiggy Wit It'?

2 What is the nationality of former World Darts Champion Raymond van Barneveld?

3 Does the Atlantic Ocean lie off the east or the west coast of South America?

4 In chemistry, which gaseous element has the smaller atomic weight, hydrogen or oxygen?

5 In which year was the UK gas industry privatised as British Gas?

6 In which century was the hormone insulin first isolated?

7 In fashion, which knee-length shorts are named after an Atlantic island?

8 In which decade was the first petrol-driven motor car made in the United Kingdom?

9 Is the 'wormwood' a type of plant or a type of insect?

10 In UK charity work, for what does the abbreviation VSO stand?

11 In Celtic folklore, which B is a spirit whose screaming is feared as an omen of impending death?

12 'Last Christmas' and 'Club Tropicana' were hits for which 1980s pop group?

13 What word can mean both a joint of ham and a German white wine?

14 In 1872, Victoria Woodhull became the first woman to run for which office in the United States of America?

15 In equestrian sport, the 'pommel', 'cantle' and 'girth' are all part of what?

16 Which of these islands is the largest, Greenland or New Guinea?

17 Kemal Ataturk was the first president of which country?

18 How many atoms of oxygen are there in one molecule of water?

19 In which year of the 1980s was Black Monday in Britain?

20 Which state in the US is nicknamed Badger State?

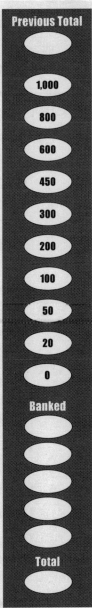

Previous Total

1,000

800

600

450

300

200

100

50

20

0

Banked

Total

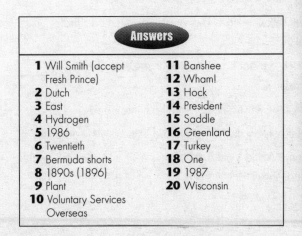

Answers

1 Will Smith (accept Fresh Prince)
2 Dutch
3 East
4 Hydrogen
5 1986
6 Twentieth
7 Bermuda shorts
8 1890s (1896)
9 Plant
10 Voluntary Services Overseas

11 Banshee
12 Wham!
13 Hock
14 President
15 Saddle
16 Greenland
17 Turkey
18 One
19 1987
20 Wisconsin

1 In which US state is the volcano Mount Saint Helen's?

2 The name of which flying dinosaurs comes from the Greek for 'wing' and 'finger'?

3 Which surname is shared by the actors Hugh and Richard E.?

4 In pop music, 'Baggy Trousers' and 'It Must Be Love' were Top 10 hits for which group?

5 In eighteenth-century Britain, the Tories were one of the main political parties. What was the other?

6 What H is the word describing a plant which dies to soil level in winter?

7 How many feet are there in ten yards?

8 In television, which British actor starred in both *The Likely Lads* and *Only When I Laugh*?

9 In which month is Europe Day celebrated?

10 Which country was known as the Dutch East Indies until 1945?

11 Which film star has won the most Oscars for Best Actress?

12 What is the longest bone in the human body?

13 In the nursery rhyme, where did Little Polly Flinders sit?

14 During World War II, the initials ARP stood for Air what Precautions?

15 Which star of the film *Seven* did Gwyneth Paltrow say was 'the sexiest man alive'?

16 The lotus flower is the national symbol of which Asian country?

17 In television, which comedy, starring Stephanie Cole, featured the rebellious residents of a retirement home?

18 In football, during 2000's charity shield game against Chelsea, which Manchester United midfielder was sent off?

19 The song 'Luck Be a Lady Tonight' comes from which musical?

20 In the honours list, what does the acronym MBE stand for?

Previous Total

1,000

800

600

450

300

200

100

50

20

0

Banked

Total

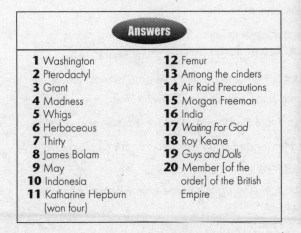

Answers

1 Washington
2 Pterodactyl
3 Grant
4 Madness
5 Whigs
6 Herbaceous
7 Thirty
8 James Bolam
9 May
10 Indonesia
11 Katharine Hepburn (won four)
12 Femur
13 Among the cinders
14 Air Raid Precautions
15 Morgan Freeman
16 India
17 *Waiting For God*
18 Roy Keane
19 *Guys and Dolls*
20 Member [of the order] of the British Empire

Round 19

1 Which island in San Francisco Bay was the site of a maximum security federal prison from 1934 to 1963?

2 If a French road sign says you are 160 kilometres from Paris, how many more miles do you need to travel to reach Paris?

3 Athletes from which country traditionally lead the parade at the opening of the Olympic Games?

4 In the animal kingdom, the whydah is a bird from which continent?

5 In geography, the island of Madeira is in which ocean?

6 In which Shakespeare play do the characters Bottom, Oberon and Puck appear?

7 In pop music, which member of Genesis had a hit in 1983 with 'You Can't Hurry Love'?

8 In the nursery rhyme, 'little boys' are made of 'slugs and snails' and what else?

9 What name is given to the art of inducing plants to produce flowers or fruit before their normal season?

10 What is the name of the Watergate-inspired film which starred Robert Redford and Dustin Hoffman?

11 Who wrote the book *Highgrove: Portrait of an Estate*?

12 Ely, Huntingdon and Peterborough are all places in which county?

13 In food, malt vinegar is made from which alcoholic liquid?

14 In 1959, which country was the first to land a man-made object on the moon?

15 In the international phonetic alphabet, if *A* is Alpha and *Z* is Zulu, what is *P*?

16 The American television comedy *Rhoda* was a spin-off from which successful series of the 1970s?

17 In pop music, which group had hits with the songs 'I'm Too Sexy' and 'Deeply Dippy'?

18 Which canal passes through the man-made lake Gatun and the Gaillard Cut?

19 What metal is mixed with copper to produce brass?

20 Which actress plays the lead in the film *Tomb Raider*?

Previous Total

( )

1,000

800

600

450

300

200

100

50

20

0

Banked

( )
( )
( )
( )
( )
( )

Total

( )

Answers

1. Alcatraz	**12** Cambridgeshire
2 100 miles	**13** Beer
3 Greece	**14** Russia (accept Soviet
4 Africa	Union or USSR)
5 Atlantic	**15** Papa
6 *A Midsummer Night's*	**16** *The Mary Tyler Moore*
Dream	*Show*
7 Phil Collins	**17** Right Said Fred
8 Puppy dogs' tails	**18** Panama Canal
9 Forcing	**19** Zinc
10 *All The President's Men*	**20** Angelina Jolie
11 Prince Charles	
(accept Charles	
Clover/[HRH] The	
Prince of Wales)	

Round 20

1 In 1966, Britain's first safari park was established in the grounds of which house?

2 In television, what kind of building was the setting for *Oh, Dr Beeching!*, starring Su Pollard?

3 By what name was Thailand known before 1939?

4 In politics, what international organisation was set up after the signing of the North Atlantic Treaty in 1949?

5 Which artist began painting characteristic scenes of his native industrial Lancashire during World War I?

6 Which American author is the creator and executive producer of the television show *ER*?

7 Who played Fred's mother-in-law in the film *The Flintstones in Viva Rock Las Vegas*?

8 In food, an 'aitchbone' is a cut of which meat?

9 Which Irish poet has published collections entitled *North*, *Field Work* and *Station Island*?

10 In clothing, where on the body would a soldier wear his busby?

11 What do crocodiles swallow both to stay underwater and to aid digestion?

12 From which country did the USA acquire Florida in 1819?

13 In the J. R. R. Tolkien novel, what type of creature is Bilbo Baggins?

14 Which fruit is used to make the type of brandy known as calvados?

15 What is the capital of Colombia?

16 In what year did Greece join the European Community, now called the European Union?

17 Which Welsh city is the home of the Millennium Stadium?

18 In which year did badminton become a medal sport at the Olympic games?

19 Which museum in Madrid contains the world's greatest collection of Spanish paintings?

20 What was the nationality of the singer Nena who reached the charts in 1984 with '99 Red Balloons'?

Previous Total

1,000

800

600

450

300

200

100

50

20

0

Banked

Total

Answers

1 Longleat (House)	**10** On his head
2 Railway station	**11** Stones/rocks
3 Siam	**12** Spain
4 NATO (or North Atlantic Treaty Organization)	**13** Hobbit
	14 Apple
5 L. S. Lowry (accept Lawrence Stephen Lowry)	**15** Bogota
	16 1981
	17 Cardiff
6 Michael Crichton (do not accept John Wells)	**18** 1992
	19 The Prado
7 Joan Collins	**20** German
8 Beef	
9 Seamus Heaney (accept Heaney)	

Round 21

1 Which darts player is nicknamed 'The Crafty Cockney'?

2 Which state covers the greatest area of land in the USA?

3 What S is a French term used to describe a spiritualist meeting?

4 Is the scientific symbol of the female a circle with a cross or with an arrow?

5 Whose films of the 1990s included *The Postman* and *Waterworld*?

6 Is the Tropic of Cancer north or south of the equator?

7 Which British country was the pop group Wet Wet Wet from?

8 Who wrote the novel *The Strange Case of Dr Jekyll and Mr Hyde*?

9 In nature, what A is the tip of the stamen that produces the pollen grains in a plant?

10 In the UK, are 0345 telephone numbers charged at local or national rate?

11 Which of these cities is furthest from London by plane: Havana or Hong Kong?

12 Was the hovercraft invented by an Englishman or a Frenchman?

13 Which B is a marine crustacean that commonly attaches itself to the hulls of ships?

14 Which gas is commonly known as laughing gas?

15 In the year 2000, which pop star announced her divorce before she had announced she was married?

16 David Lloyd George was the last British prime minister to be a leader of which party?

17 In sport, on what would you find a 'point', a 'barrel' and a 'flight'?

18 Complete the title of this Cole Porter song, 'Let's Do . . .' what?

19 If you were travelling on a wagon-lit, how would you be travelling?

20 In television, Timothy West played Bradley Hardacre in which comedy series of the 1980s?

Previous Total

1,000

800

600

450

300

200

100

50

20

0

Banked

Total

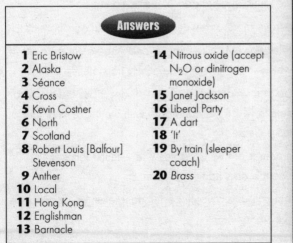

Answers

1 Eric Bristow
2 Alaska
3 Séance
4 Cross
5 Kevin Costner
6 North
7 Scotland
8 Robert Louis [Balfour] Stevenson
9 Anther
10 Local
11 Hong Kong
12 Englishman
13 Barnacle

14 Nitrous oxide (accept N_2O or dinitrogen monoxide)
15 Janet Jackson
16 Liberal Party
17 A dart
18 'It'
19 By train (sleeper coach)
20 Brass

1 In a US postal address, MN is the abbreviation for which state?

2 In which century did Colley Cibber become the English Poet Laureate?

3 What M is a large tent, or a canopy over the entrance to a building?

4 Who played James Bond in *For Your Eyes Only* and *Live And Let Die*?

5 In cookery, when using a pestle and mortar, which is the bowl?

6 With which garden flower is George Russell, who grew them on allotments in York, particularly associated: lupins or tulips?

7 In biology, the stirrup is the common name for a small bone found in what part of the human head?

8 Are there more or fewer than four litres in one gallon?

9 In television, Michael Elphick and Angela Thorne starred in which sitcom about two unlikely flatmates?

10 In politics, what four-word phrase describes the electoral system in which the candidate with the highest number of votes is elected?

11 The names of two US states end with the letter *T*. Vermont is one, name the other.

12 What colour is a youth hostel triangle on an Ordnance Survey map?

13 What colour is the Star of David on the Israeli flag?

14 In the animal kingdom, albacore is a variety of which edible fish?

15 In pop music, 'In the Navy' was a hit for which American group of the 1970s?

16 Hamburg and Hanover are cities in which country?

17 With what sport would you associate Jean Alesi?

18 Does the Pacific Ocean lie off the east or the west coast of South America?

19 In how many *Rocky* films has Sylvester Stallone appeared?

20 Pertussis is the medical name for which childhood disease, mumps or whooping cough?

Previous Total

1,000
800
600
450
300
200
100
50
20
0

Banked

Total

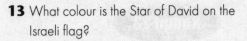

Answers

1 Minnesota	**12** Pink (accept red)
2 Eighteenth century (1730)	**13** Blue
3 Marquee	**14** Tuna
4 Roger Moore	**15** Village People
5 Mortar	**16** Germany
6 Lupins	**17** Motor racing (accept Grand Prix/motor sports/Formula One)
7 Middle ear (accept ear)	**18** West
8 More	**19** Five
9 *Three Up Two Down*	**20** Whooping cough
10 First past the post	
11 Connecticut	

Round 23

1 In which English city is the Central School of Speech and Drama?

2 Until 1918, Austria was joined in a dual monarchy with which country?

3 In science, does alkaline soil have a pH level greater or less than 6 or 7?

4 Which John Grisham novel was turned into a film in 1994 starring Susan Sarandon?

5 In poetry, did Ted Hughes or Cecil Day Lewis become the English Poet Laureate first?

6 Which animal has the Latin name *Bufo bufo*: a toad or a cat?

7 Which Englishwoman became notorious in 1963 for revealing her affairs with a Soviet naval attaché and the English secretary of state for war?

8 In astrology, in which two months could you have been born if your star sign was Sagittarius?

9 In which year was the Berlin Wall erected?

10 In football, which Arsenal midfielder was sent off in his first two Premiership games in the 2000/2001 season?

11 In which decade did Richard Branson complete his first crossing of the Atlantic in a hot-air balloon?

12 In film, which cast member of *The Godfather* refused to accept his Oscar?

13 In terms of land area, is the Republic of Ireland or England larger?

14 Which B is a South American nut, also known as the 'Pará nut' or 'cream nut' because of its flavour?

15 In the periodic table, which chemical symbol represents neon?

16 In the television soap *EastEnders*, how is Pauline Fowler related to Ian Beale?

17 Which country's players have dominated world table tennis since the 1980s?

18 In pop music, which girl group scored its first number one with 'Never Ever'?

19 What was the first name of the Czech novelist Kafka, who was born in 1883?

20 What type of camera, which produces instantaneous prints, was invented in the late 1940s?

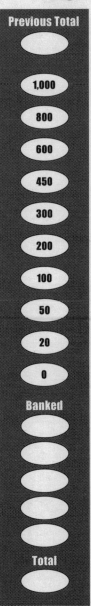

Previous Total

1,000
800
600
450
300
200
100
50
20
0

Banked

Total

Answers

1 London	**12** Marlon Brando
2 Hungary	**13** England
3 Greater	**14** Brazil nut
4 *The Client*	**15** Ne
5 Cecil Day Lewis	**16** His aunt
6 Toad	**17** China (accept People's Republic of China)
7 Christine Keeler	
8 November and December	**18** All Saints
9 1961	**19** Franz
10 Patrick Viera	**20** Polaroid
11 1980s (1987)	

Round 24

1 In the UK, what is traditionally given as a gift on the fifteenth wedding anniversary?

2 Which cartoon show was turned into the film *Bigger, Longer & Uncut* in 1999?

3 In politics, what is the German equivalent of the post of prime minister?

4 In seamanship, the 'bowline', 'figure-eight' and 'reef' are all types of what?

5 In which country is Copacabana Beach?

6 In the Paper, Scissors, Stone game, what wins over Paper?

7 Which English princess became a pupil at St George's School, Ascot, in September 2000?

8 How many scientific units are denoted by the prefix 'mega'?

9 In the Bible, who was given a richly ornamented robe by his father Jacob?

10 In New York City, which borough is north-east of the Harlem River and home to the New York Zoological Society?

11 Which musical features the character Daddy Warbucks?

12 In food, which vegetable's name comes from the Latin for 'flowered cabbage'?

13 In football, Mark Venus of Ipswich Town was the first player to do what in the Premiership in the 2000/2001 season?

14 In astrology, which sign falls between the star signs of Pisces and Taurus?

15 Which American author won the Nobel Prize for Literature in 1962?

16 In gardening, 'checkerboard' is a variety of which flower?

17 In maths, if a train travels at 80 miles per hour, how far does it go in two and a quarter hours?

18 Stanley is the capital of which group of islands in the South Atlantic Ocean?

19 In the animal kingdom, a 'gosling' is a young what?

20 In nature, what T describes the loss of water from a plant's leaves through tiny holes?

Previous Total

1,000
800
600
450
300
200
100
50
20
0

Banked

Total

Round 25

1 Which American state is known as the 'Equality State' because it was the first in the world to give full voting rights to women?

2 In nature, what is a monkey puzzle?

3 In maths, how many feet are there in one hundred yards?

4 In the television sitcom *2 Point 4 Children*, what is the surname of the family?

5 In which Thomas Hardy novel are Gabriel Oak and Sergeant Troy rivals for the hand of Bathsheba Everdene?

6 Complete this quote by Albert Einstein: 'God does not play . . .' what?

7 Which child star sang the song 'On the Good Ship Lollipop' in 1934?

8 Abyssinia is the former name of which country?

9 In history, which bridge, named after a mythological flying horse, was the first to be captured on D-Day?

10 Two branches of which tree appear on the national flag of Cyprus?

11 In television, what was Yosser Hughes's catchphrase in *Boys From The Blackstuff*?

12 What *X* is a percussion instrument played by striking a row of wooden bars with small beaters?

13 On which gymnastics apparatus might one see a Tsukahara performed?

14 'The Rain in Spain' is a song from which musical?

15 In clothing, what kind of garment is a 'bomber'?

16 In UK finance, what does the *P* stand for in the acronym PAYE?

17 In the UK, which licence cost 37 pence when it was abolished in 1988?

18 In film, whose portrayal of Wall Street shark Gordon Gekko won him an Oscar for Best Actor?

19 Cape Wrath is a headland at the north-west tip of which country?

20 Josephine and Marie Louise were the two wives of which French leader?

Answers

1 Wyoming	**11** 'Gissa job'
2 A tree (accept evergreen tree, conifer, Chile pine, Araucaria)	**12** Xylophone
	13 Horse vault/vault/vaulting horse
3 Three hundred	**14** *My Fair Lady*
4 Porter	**15** Jacket
5 *Far From the Madding Crowd*	**16** Pay
	17 Dog licence
6 Dice	**18** Michael Douglas
7 Shirley Temple	**19** Scotland
8 Ethiopia	**20** Emperor Napoleon [I, or Bonaparte]
9 Pegasus Bridge	
10 Olive	

Round 26

1 In the animal kingdom, the 'Russian blue' is a breed of which domestic animal?

2 What nationality was the playwright Joe Orton?

3 In pop music, what was the title of Men At Work's worldwide hit song about Australia?

4 Which British statesman's 1955 portrait by artist Graham Sutherland was destroyed after his death on the instructions of his widow?

5 Which Disney character plays the Sorcerer's Apprentice in the film *Fantasia*?

6 In David Lynch's film *The Straight Story*, what is Alvin Straight's preferred mode of transport?

7 In which decade did Professor Rubik of Hungary invent his cube?

8 Who presented a 1988 television documentary on architecture called *A Vision of Britain*?

9 In drinks, which mixer, sometimes used with vodka or gin, contains quinine?

10 Which creatures suddenly and mysteriously died out at the end of the Mesozoic era?

11 Which planet in our solar system is the most similar to Venus in terms of size and mass?

12 What is the only mammal to achieve true flight?

13 On television, which character did Patrick Macnee play in *The Avengers* and *The New Avengers*?

14 *Notes From a Big Country* is a book by Bill Bryson about which country?

15 Which female singer had hits in 1993 with 'Dreams' and in the year 2000 with 'Rise'?

16 In maths, if the time is 9.40 a.m., how many minutes must pass before it is midday?

17 Which founder member of the SDP was elected chancellor of Oxford University in March 1987?

18 In English law, a divorce decree that brings a marriage to a legal end is a decree what?

19 In English history, which M . . . C . . . did King John seal in 1215?

20 What is the first name of Jane and Peter Fonda's actor father?

Previous Total

1,000

800

600

450

300

200

100

50

20

0

Banked

Total

Answers

1 Cat
2 English (accept British)
3 'Down Under'
4 Sir Winston Churchill's
5 Mickey Mouse
6 Lawnmower
7 1970s (1975)
8 [HRH] Prince Charles (Prince of Wales)
9 Tonic [water]
10 Dinosaurs
11 Earth
12 Bat

13 [John] Steed
14 USA (accept America)
15 Gabrielle
16 140 minutes
17 Lord Jenkins [of Hillhead] (accept Roy Jenkins)
18 Absolute
19 Magna Carta
20 Henry

Round 27

1 In 1980s pop music, which of Ultravox's songs was held off the number one spot by Joe Dolce's 'Shaddap You Face'?

2 Which author wrote the novel *The Odessa File*?

3 Which ship canal, running inland from the Mersey Estuary, was constructed between 1887 and 1894?

4 What is the title of Mike Leigh's Oscar-winning film about Gilbert and Sullivan?

5 In which country did the Klondike Gold Rush of 1896 take place?

6 Which composer, whose name was used by a popular singer of the 1960s, wrote the music for the opera *Hansel And Gretel*?

7 Turin and Bologna are cities in which country?

8 In which North African country was French author Albert Camus born?

9 Which child music prodigy played the harpsichord for George III at the age of eight?

10 Which Andrew Lloyd Webber musical features the song 'The Music of the Night'?

11 In politics, what, in the context of parliamentary elections, do the letters STV stand for?

12 The UK, Denmark and which other country joined the EEC in 1973?

13 In food, a dish described as 'carbonade' is beef cooked in which alcoholic beverage?

14 In pop music, from which African country is the group Ladysmith Black Mambazo?

15 Is the Walker Art Gallery in Liverpool or Manchester?

16 Sir Rowland Hill, author of the 1837 book *Post Office Reform*, created what?

17 Which flower is the national symbol of the Netherlands?

18 In medicine, which is worse, a first-degree burn or a third-degree burn?

19 What nationality is Paul Hogan, star of the *Crocodile Dundee* films?

20 In the animal kingdom, is the anaconda snake native to North or South America?

Previous Total

1,000

800

600

450

300

200

100

50

20

0

Banked

Total

Answers

1 'Vienna'	**11** Single transferable vote
2 Frederick Forsythe	**12** [Republic of] Ireland
3 Manchester Ship Canal	**13** Beer
4 *Topsy-Turvy*	**14** South Africa
5 Canada	**15** Liverpool
6 Engelbert Humperdinck	**16** The postage stamp
7 Italy	**17** Tulip
8 Algeria	**18** Third-degree burn
9 [Wolfgang Amadeus] Mozart	**19** Australian
10 *The Phantom of the Opera*	**20** South America

Round 28

1 Which actor played Batman in the 1997 film *Batman and Robin*?

2 Sparta was an ancient city-state in which modern country?

3 In maths, what is six times seven?

4 In which Commonwealth country are the governor general, the prime minister and the leader of the opposition all women: Australia or New Zealand?

5 What *H* is the name given to a group of buffalo or bison?

6 In film, how many times did Timothy Dalton play James Bond?

7 In history, what game did British and German soldiers play during the Christmas Day truce in 1914?

8 Which literary prize did Winston Churchill win in 1953?

9 Who was the only American president to resign in office in the twentieth century?

10 What is the current UK telephone dialling code for Leeds?

11 Which Roman emperor was the subject of two novels by Robert Graves?

12 What *F* is an establishment where metals are cast in moulds?

13 In the nursery rhyme, give the line which usually follows 'Old King Cole was a merry old soul'.

14 In geography, does China share its border with more or fewer than ten countries?

15 In which decade was the singer Freddie Mercury born?

16 Which type of transport was preferred by the 'Two Fat Ladies' in their television cookery series?

17 Which former general became president of France in 1958?

18 In ancient history, Caesarion was the son of Julius Caesar and which queen?

19 In maths, a nonagon is a shape with how many sides?

20 In the animal kingdom, does a badger walk with its feet pointing inwards or outwards?

Previous Total

◯

1,000

800

600

450

300

200

100

50

20

0

Banked

◯
◯
◯
◯
◯

Total

◯

Answers

1 George Clooney	**11** Claudius
2 Greece	**12** Foundry
3 42	**13** 'And a merry old soul
4 New Zealand	was he'
5 Herd	**14** More
6 Twice (*The Living Daylights* and *Licence To Kill*)	**15** 1940s (1946)
7 Football (accept soccer)	**16** Motorbike and sidecar (accept just motorcycle/motorbike)
8 Nobel Prize for Literature	**17** [Charles] de Gaulle
9 [Richard] Nixon	**18** Cleopatra
10 0113	**19** Nine
	20 Inwards

Round 29

1 In biology, what is the largest organ inside the human body?

2 In which decade was London's post office tower, now called the British Telecom tower, opened?

3 In science, what G is the name given to a small opening on the Earth's surface that periodically spouts a fountain of boiling water and steam?

4 Which star of musicals was born Elaine Bickerstaff?

5 In cookery, what are dried plums usually called?

6 Which title, meaning emperor, was held by the German ruler Wilhelm II?

7 Television comic Bernie Clifton is famous for riding which comedy bird?

8 Which English county is also a forename of the author Maugham?

9 The parliament of which of the British Isles is called Tynwald?

10 In nutrition, is riboflavin a form of vitamin A or vitamin B?

11 In history, how many tsars of Russia have been called Nicholas?

12 In literature, did Nick Hornby write the book *About a Boy* or *Man and Boy*?

13 Which leading man appeared in the films *On The Waterfront*, *The Godfather* and *Apocalypse Now*?

14 Complete the title of the Willy Russell play *Educating . . .* who?

15 How many darts does each player use in a standard game?

16 Which children's game is played using the fruit of the horse chestnut tree?

17 In the animal kingdom, is the jellyfish a member of the fish family?

18 Is the ski resort of Zermatt in Germany or Switzerland?

19 The 1965 film *The Collector* is based on whose novel?

20 Which English Premiership football team is nicknamed 'The Gunners'?

Previous Total

( )

1,000

800

600

450

300

200

100

50

20

0

Banked

Total

( )

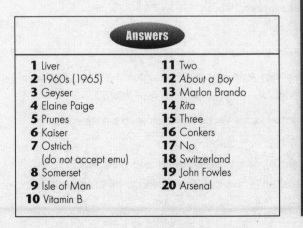

Answers

1 Liver	**11** Two
2 1960s (1965)	**12** *About a Boy*
3 Geyser	**13** Marlon Brando
4 Elaine Paige	**14** *Rita*
5 Prunes	**15** Three
6 Kaiser	**16** Conkers
7 Ostrich	**17** No
(*do not* accept emu)	**18** Switzerland
8 Somerset	**19** John Fowles
9 Isle of Man	**20** Arsenal
10 Vitamin B	

Round 30

1 Central and Queen Street are the main railway terminals in which Scottish city?

2 Which Peter Benchley novel, published in 1974, is about a town terrorised by a shark?

3 In maths, what is 3 multiplied by 9?

4 In the animal kingdom, a Duroc is a type of what animal?

5 In music, what was the first of Madonna's songs to reach the UK number one spot: 'Holiday' or 'Into the Groove'?

6 In England, in which month is Remembrance Sunday?

7 The childhood of which deaf and blind woman is the subject of the famous play *The Miracle Worker*?

8 In which decade were parking meters introduced into the UK?

9 Which country's so-called October Revolution started on 7 November 1917?

10 What is the current UK telephone dialling code for Newcastle upon Tyne?

11 Who was American president throughout the Second World War, until his death in April 1945?

12 In nature, is the yucca plant native to the Americas or Africa?

13 In architecture, is the perpendicular style, which flourished in England, considered to be Gothic or Georgian?

14 In how many *Lethal Weapon* films have Mel Gibson and Danny Glover appeared together?

15 What N is the name of the valley north of San Francisco which is an important area for grape growing and wine production?

16 First manufactured by Colman's at Newry, County Down, in 1946, 'Pom' was the first brand of instant what to be sold in Britain?

17 In pop music, which group had hits with 'Radio Gaga' and 'I Want to Break Free'?

18 In which decade did the ship the *QE2* make her maiden voyage?

19 The oil of which spice is traditionally used as a cure for toothache?

20 If a person is 'pigeon-toed', do their feet turn inwards or outwards?

Previous Total

1,000

800

600

450

300

200

100

50

20

0

Banked

Total

Answers

1 Glasgow	**12** The Americas
2 Jaws	**13** Gothic
3 27	**14** Four
4 Pig	**15** Napa Valley
5 'Into the Groove'	**16** Mashed potato (accept mash)
6 November	**17** Queen
7 Helen Keller	**18** 1960s
8 1950s	**19** Cloves
9 Russia	**20** Inwards
10 0191	
11 Franklin [Delano] Roosevelt	

Round 31

1 What is the largest freshwater lake in Great Britain?

2 Used in technical drawing, what shape is a 'set square'?

3 What type of dwelling shares its name with a group of camels?

4 In nature, is larkspur the name of a plant or a bird?

5 In which decade did Israel fight the so-called Yom Kippur War: the 1960s or 1970s?

6 Which ex-Spice Girl released an album called *Schizophonic*?

7 Haarlem and The Hague are cities in which country?

8 J. D. Salinger's novel *The Catcher in the Rye* is set in which country?

9 In space exploration, what name is given to the moment a space rocket leaves the launch pad?

10 In nature, is the aspen an evergreen or a deciduous tree?

11 Which French saint led a battle against the English and was burned in 1431 for witchcraft?

12 In film, Jim Carrey played which pet detective?

13 How many weeks does a standard human pregnancy last?

14 In art, whose best-known paintings, *Primavera* and *The Birth of Venus*, can be seen at the Uffizi Gallery in his native Florence?

15 In television, which comedy duo starred as *Jeeves and Wooster*?

16 Which Hollywood star became the Princess of Monaco?

17 In language, what does the Italian word 'donna' mean?

18 In Britain, which fine cut of beef is found between the rump and the forerib?

19 In the animal kingdom, is the Bald Eagle really bald?

20 When did the Post Office introduce British postal codes: 1958 or 1968?

Previous Total

1,000

800

600

450

300

200

100

50

20

0

Banked

Total

Answers

1 Loch Lomond
2 Triangle/triangular
3 Caravan
4 Plant
5 1970s (1973)
6 Geri Halliwell (accept Ginger Spice)
7 The Netherlands/Holland
8 United States (accept also USA, America)
9 Lift-off (accept blast-off)
10 Deciduous
11 Joan of Arc (accept also St Joan/Maid of Orleans/La Pucelle d'Orleans/Jeanne d'Arc)
12 Ace Ventura
13 40 weeks
14 [Sandro] Botticelli (accept Alessandro di Mariano Filipepi)
15 Stephen Fry and Hugh Laurie
16 Grace Kelly
17 Woman (lady, madam)
18 Sirloin
19 No
20 1958

Round 32

1 Which was the first to be advertised on television in 1955, toothpaste or shampoo?

2 In sport, has the Grand National been run for more or less than 100 years?

3 In biology, which organ removes waste material from the blood?

4 Palma is the capital of which of Spain's Balearic Islands?

5 In film, who directed *A Nightmare on Elm Street* and the *Scream* horror series?

6 What is the most northerly town of the British Isles?

7 Which part of the basil plant is used to flavour food?

8 In the business world, what is the name of the organisation represented by the initials CBI?

9 Which common breed of black-and-white dairy cattle was introduced from the Netherlands early in the twentieth century?

10 In what decade was the television programme *Match of the Day* first broadcast?

11 Complete this song title from the musical *Paint Your Wagon*: 'I was born under . . .' what?

12 In music, what was the title of the Mamas And The Papas' debut hit?

13 In medicine, lumbago directly affects which part of the human body?

14 Which was the first West African country to win independence from the UK: Ghana or Nigeria?

15 In fashion, which M is a maker of women's hats and headwear?

16 In pop music, in the 1950s, who had a UK number one hit with 'Dreamboat': Lita Roza or Alma Cogan?

17 In theatre, which type of party makes the title of a Harold Pinter play?

18 Which Roman general was known to his countrymen as 'Marcus Antonius'?

19 In the children's television series, which Teletubby has a scooter?

20 Tiger Bay is an area in which British city?

Previous Total

1,000

800

600

450

300

200

100

50

20

0

Banked

Total

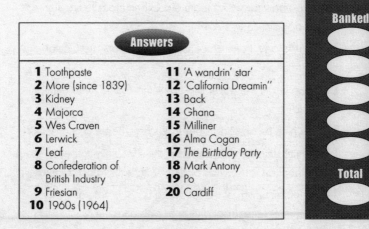

Answers

1 Toothpaste	**11** 'A wandrin' star'
2 More (since 1839)	**12** 'California Dreamin''
3 Kidney	**13** Back
4 Majorca	**14** Ghana
5 Wes Craven	**15** Milliner
6 Lerwick	**16** Alma Cogan
7 Leaf	**17** *The Birthday Party*
8 Confederation of	**18** Mark Antony
British Industry	**19** Po
9 Friesian	**20** Cardiff
10 1960s (1964)	

Round 33

1 In politics, who resigned as the Conservative candidate for London mayor and was replaced by Steve Norris?

2 How many players are there on the pitch in a rugby league team at the start of a game?

3 In bingo, which number is traditionally called as 'two fat ladies'?

4 Which high-security prison is located in a national park in Devon and was originally built to house French prisoners during the Napoleonic Wars?

5 In the 1960s, which country launched the Gemini space programme?

6 Which US president said, 'Read my lips, no new taxes,' during his campaign in 1989?

7 Pop singer David Robert Jones is better known by which stage name?

8 In travel, which resort is known as 'the Mexican Riviera'?

9 In football, for which team did Glenn Hoddle first sign as an apprentice in 1974?

10 In astrology, in which constellation of stars are Castor and Pollux?

11 Who wrote the novel *The Spy Who Came in from the Cold*?

12 In which British soap opera was Pete Beale a character?

13 Which actress, who starred in the 1955 film *Rebel Without a Cause*, was originally called Natasha Gurdin?

14 In nature, which of the following is not a naturally occurring fibre: abaca, flax or abalone?

15 In chess, which piece has the combined powers of the rook and the bishop?

16 Which author wrote the book *Spycatcher*, published in 1987?

17 The United Kingdom's Clean Air Act of 1956 was an attempt to get rid of what form of pollution?

18 In politics, who were given full voting rights by the Nineteenth Amendment to the American Constitution?

19 Which American pop duo wrote and recorded a number of songs for the film *The Graduate*?

20 For which British singer was the musical *Half a Sixpence* written?

Previous Total

1,000

800

600

450

300

200

100

50

20

0

Banked

Total

Answers

1 Lord Archer/Jeffrey Archer

2 13

3 88

4 Dartmoor prison (accept Dartmoor)

5 USA

6 George Bush (do not accept George Bush, Jr)

7 David Bowie (accept Ziggy Stardust)

8 Acapulco

9 Tottenham Hotspur (accept Spurs)

10 Gemini

11 John le Carré (accept David Cornwell)

12 *EastEnders*

13 Natalie Wood

14 Abalone

15 Queen

16 Peter Wright

17 Smog (accept smoky fog)

18 Women

19 [Paul] Simon and [Art] Garfunkel

20 Tommy Steele

Round 34

1 Which eighteenth-century explorer was able to show that the 'great southern continent' did not exist?

2 With which musical instrument is Jools Holland usually associated?

3 In medicine, the condition of alopecia involves the loss of what?

4 In the 1719 classic novel, what is the first name of the castaway Crusoe?

5 Which is the oldest college at Cambridge University?

6 Which white-berried parasitic plant was regarded as sacred by the ancient druids?

7 Charles Lindbergh was the first person to fly solo across which ocean in his plane, *The Spirit of St Louis*?

8 What nationality is the playwright Harold Pinter?

9 In which year was snowboarding first included in the Winter Olympics?

10 In history, which German state was once ruled by 'Mad King Ludwig', best known today for his extravagant buildings?

11 In the Bible, how many books are there in the standard New Testament?

12 Which film saw Roger Moore's first big screen appearance as 007?

13 'Heliophobia' is a morbid fear of which heavenly body?

14 The city of Gothenburg is in which country?

15 In what century was slavery officially abolished in the British Empire?

16 Which Jamaican holiday spot is also the island's second-largest city?

17 In television, Paul Michael Glaser and David Soul played which 1970s detectives?

18 Who received the Pulitzer Prize in 1983 for her novel *The Color Purple*?

19 With which school subject are the Fibonacci sequence and Pascal's triangle associated?

20 In sport, what is the nationality of the year 2000 Tour de France winner, Lance Armstrong?

Previous Total

1,000

800

600

450

300

200

100

50

20

0

Banked

Total

Answers

1 James Cook	**12** *Live and Let Die*
2 Piano/keyboards	**13** The sun
3 Hair	**14** Sweden
4 Robinson	**15** Nineteenth
5 Peterhouse (1284)	**16** Montego Bay
6 Mistletoe	**17** [Dave] Starsky and
7 Atlantic Ocean	[Ken] Hutch[inson]
8 English (accept British)	**18** Alice Walker
9 1998	**19** Mathematics
10 Bavaria	**20** American
11 27	

Round 35

1 In geography, what name is given to the Atlantic region infamous for apparently strange disappearances of ships and planes?

2 Which stage and film musical tells the story of Sally Bowles and the Kit Kat Klub?

3 Montezuma was the last emperor of which Central American ancient civilisation?

4 Which British comic regularly features Roger the Dodger?

5 In pop music, Believe was a 1998 album by which female singer?

6 In the first Star Wars film, what was the name of Han Solo's spaceship?

7 Which member of the royal family is director of production for the television company Ardent Productions Limited?

8 In biology, what F is the soft spot on a baby's head?

9 In Christian religion, who was the author of the third gospel and the Acts of the Apostles?

10 In golf, who was the first European ever to win the US Masters?

11 What was the first name of Lister, the pioneer of antiseptic surgery?

12 Which precious stone is traditionally given as a gift on the 40th wedding anniversary?

13 In the animal kingdom, how many species of zebra are there?

14 In television, which shabbily dressed detective was played by Peter Falk?

15 Which of the British armed forces has a training college in Dartmouth?

16 In the Bible, who is the wife of Abraham and the mother of Isaac?

17 Who was the first man to sail non-stop, single-handed, around the world?

18 In literature, J. R. R. Tolkien's *The Hobbit* is the prelude to which three-volume novel?

19 In pop music, with which band did Paul Weller have his first number one single?

20 In sport, Shirley Crabtree was better known as which television wrestler?

Previous Total

◯

1,000

800

600

450

300

200

100

50

20

0

Banked

◯

◯

◯

◯

◯

Total

◯

Answers

1 Bermuda Triangle
2 *Cabaret*
3 Aztecs
4 *The Beano*
5 Cher
6 *Millennium Falcon*
7 [HRH] Prince Edward [Earl of Wessex]
8 Fontanelle
9 St Luke
10 Severiano Ballesteros (accept Seve Ballesteros)
11 Joseph
12 Ruby
13 Three
14 [Lieutenant Philip] Columbo
15 Navy
16 Sarah (accept Sarai)
17 Robin Knox-Johnston
18 *The Lord of the Rings*
19 The Jam
20 Big Daddy

Round 36

1 How many 'cities of culture' were designated by the European Union in the year 2000?

2 On 31 December of which year did the last National Servicemen receive their call-up papers?

3 In the animal kingdom, does each housefly's life cycle begin as an egg or a maggot?

4 Which English city is the home of the G-Mex exhibition centre?

5 In the 1980s, which Scotsman was twice world darts champion?

6 Which meat, along with butter and sugar, was the first commodity to be rationed in 1940, at the start of World War II?

7 Is the Republic of Ghana situated in northern or western Africa?

8 In the Bible, what was the name of King David's wife who was previously married to Nabal: Abigail or Anna?

9 In nature, which gas is produced by photosynthesis, oxygen or nitrogen?

10 In nature, a hairstreak is a variety of which insect?

11 In literature, complete the title of the Arthur Ransome children's story: *Swallows and . . .* what?

12 In fashion, what type of clothing is a poncho?

13 Which of these cities is furthest from London by plane: Seoul or Toronto?

14 In pop music, who was vice-president of Motown records and also the lead singer of the Miracles?

15 On the internet, does the term 'Telnet' refer to information found on bulletin boards, or to remote computer access?

16 In literature, what nationality was Anthony Burgess, the author of *A Clockwork Orange*?

17 Which British politician gave the infamous 'rivers of blood' speech in April 1968?

18 In which action film did Tom Cruise first play the character Ethan Hunt?

19 In sport, in which position does the England footballer David Seaman play?

20 In the traditional story, which child is eaten by a wolf disguised as an old woman?

Previous Total

1,000

800

600

450

300

200

100

50

20

0

Banked

Total

Answers

1 Nine
2 1960
3 Egg (which hatches into a maggot)
4 Manchester
5 Jocky Wilson
6 Bacon/ham
7 Western
8 Abigail
9 Oxygen
10 Butterfly
11 *Amazons*
12 Cloak/coat/shawl/ cape/blanket with a hole for the head
13 Seoul
14 Smokey Robinson
15 Remote computer access
16 English (accept British)
17 Enoch Powell
18 *Mission Impossible* (do not accept MI2)
19 Goalkeeper
20 *Little Red Riding Hood*

Round 37

1 In history, who crowned Napoleon Bonaparte emperor of France in 1804?

2 In geography, are the Great Smoky Mountains in Canada or the USA?

3 In literature, which annual race event features in Enid Bagnold's novel *National Velvet*?

4 In architecture, did the Palladian style evolve in Italy or Spain?

5 Lausanne and Lucerne are cities in which country?

6 The Munchkins are characters from which famous film starring Judy Garland?

7 Which building is taller, the Eiffel Tower or Rouen Cathedral?

8 In food, scrag end is a cut of which meat?

9 The pop bands Big Country and Deacon Blue both come from which part of the UK?

10 The dismantling of which infamous German structure began in November 1989?

11 In nature, what does a mole prefer to eat: grass or earthworms?

12 In maths, isosceles and scalene are both forms of which plane shape?

13 Which superhero's foes included Mister Freeze and The Penguin?

14 In physics, what F is the pivot or fixed point on which a lever moves?

15 Before Bill Clinton, how many presidents of the United States had been impeached?

16 In geography, to which island group does the island of Herm belong?

17 In the animal kingdom, how many eyes does a caterpillar have, six or twelve?

18 The city of Krakow is in which country?

19 In literature, who narrates Arthur Conan Doyle's Sherlock Holmes stories?

20 In 1994, which country won football's World Cup for the fourth time?

Previous Total

( )

1,000

800

600

450

300

200

100

50

20

0

Banked

( )

( )

( )

( )

( )

Total

( )

Answers

1 Himself
2 USA
3 Grand National (accept horseracing/ steeplechasing)
4 Italy
5 [Confederation of] Switzerland
6 *The Wizard of Oz*
7 Eiffel Tower
8 Lamb/mutton
9 Scotland
10 Berlin Wall
11 Earthworms
12 Triangle
13 Batman/the Batman
14 Fulcrum
15 One (Andrew Johnson in 1868)
16 Channel Islands
17 Twelve
18 Poland
19 [Dr John H.] Watson
20 Brazil

Round 38

1 Which Joan made her film debut in *Lady Godiva Rides Again* in 1951?

2 In science, the gas radon is given off by which element, whose symbol is Rn?

3 The Securitate were the secret police of which Eastern European country?

4 In pop music, name the a cappella group who had a Christmas number one in 1983 with 'Only You'.

5 In English geography, at the mouth of which river does Sunderland stand: the Wear or the Tees?

6 Which foodstuff is sold as small, medium, large or very large, now that the 1–7 sizing system has been abolished?

7 Which West End musical has the cast performing on roller skates?

8 In rock music, John Francis Bongiovi, Jr is better known by which name?

9 In which town on the outskirts of Paris was the peace treaty signed after World War I?

10 In literature, Bernice Rubens won which prize in 1970 for the book *The Elected Member*?

11 In the animal kingdom, what is the name given to the offspring of a pen and a cob?

12 In politics, which British prime minister brought in the 'three-day week' in 1973?

13 In astrology, which star sign falls between the star signs of Libra and Sagittarius?

14 Jockey Sir Gordon Richards won which horse race in 1953, at his 28th attempt?

15 What C name is given to the French brandy which has been distilled twice?

16 In geology, a palaeontologist studies what, that are found in rocks?

17 When correctly spelt, does the letter *I* come before or after *E* in the word 'weird'?

18 What is the name of the largest cut diamond in existence?

19 In the television series of the same name, what type of business did Steptoe and Son operate?

20 Which English Premiership football team features a cannon on its club badge?

Previous Total

1,000

800

600

450

300

200

100

50

20

0

Banked

Total

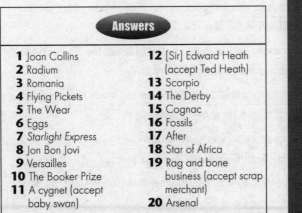

Answers

1 Joan Collins	**12** [Sir] Edward Heath
2 Radium	(accept Ted Heath)
3 Romania	**13** Scorpio
4 Flying Pickets	**14** The Derby
5 The Wear	**15** Cognac
6 Eggs	**16** Fossils
7 *Starlight Express*	**17** After
8 Jon Bon Jovi	**18** Star of Africa
9 Versailles	**19** Rag and bone
10 The Booker Prize	business (accept scrap
11 A cygnet (accept	merchant)
baby swan)	**20** Arsenal

Round 39

1 In the title of Samuel Beckett's play, who was being waited for?

2 In countries such as Saudi Arabia, desalination plants are built to provide supplies of what?

3 From what country did the inventor of cellophane, Dr Jaques Edwin Brandenburger, come?

4 In the animal kingdom, which mountain range is the natural habitat of the llama?

5 In what decade was the Thames Flood Barrier completed?

6 The name of which Roman goddess is used as a general term for the plant life of a region?

7 Which amusement park opened near Stoke-on-Trent in 1979?

8 Which star of BBC Television's comedy series *The Royle Family* is reputedly set to join Hollywood actor Samuel L. Jackson in the film *The 51st State*?

9 In history, was it in 1716 or 1816 that the first steamship crossed the English Channel?

10 Which political party has a name which means, in English, the Party of Wales?

11 In sport, which London football team had a chart hit in 1981 with the song 'Ossie's Dream'?

12 Mumbai is the official name of an Indian city. By what name is it generally known?

13 The ancient Etruscan civilisation once flourished in which modern country?

14 On the World Wide Web, what country does '.dk' represent?

15 In which American city is Georgetown University?

16 In food, what *B* is the main ingredient in the Middle Eastern salad dish tabbouleh?

17 In sport, who was the first Australian cricketer to be knighted?

18 In astrology, the star sign Virgo is represented by what image?

19 Who was the author of the novel *The Carpetbaggers*?

20 Which is the largest wild carnivore native to Britain, often called 'brock'?

Previous Total

1,000

800

600

450

300

200

100

50

20

0

Banked

Total

Answers

1 Godot
2 Fresh water (by taking salt from sea water)
3 Switzerland
4 Andes
5 1980s
6 Flora
7 Alton Towers
8 Ricky Tomlinson
9 1816 (a paddleboat)
10 Plaid Cymru
11 Tottenham Hotspur (accept Spurs)
12 Bombay
13 Italy
14 Denmark
15 Washington, DC
16 Bulgur wheat (do *not* accept just wheat)
17 Sir Donald Bradman
18 A virgin (accept girl/young woman/maiden/harvest maiden)
19 Harold Robbins
20 Badger

Round 40

1 Hugh Grant stars in which film, adapted from Helen Fielding's bestselling British novel?

2 In sport, which English Midlands football team is nicknamed 'The Sky Blues'?

3 Which Spanish singer's version of 'Begin the Beguine' topped the UK charts in 1981?

4 In the animal kingdom, which creature makes the loudest noises, capable of being detected 500 miles away?

5 In literature, what nationality was the falcon in the title of Dashiell Hammett's novel?

6 In politics, what name is given to the electoral system in which the number of seats gained by a party directly reflects their total overall vote?

7 By what name is the politician William Jefferson Blythe the Fourth better known?

8 The former Royal Yacht *Britannia* is now a tourist attraction in which Scottish city?

9 How many hours are there in three days?

10 In literature, what A is a condensed or shortened version of a work?

11 In science, what is extracted from a substance for it to be described as 'anhydrous'?

12 Which pop band had a UK hit in 1995 with 'Country House'?

13 In Eric Carle's children's book, what is Very Hungry?

14 What is the first name of the former German Chancellor Kohl?

15 Name the Irish singer who had a hit with 'Orinoco Flow'.

16 In which musical does the song 'Sit Down, You're Rockin' the Boat' appear?

17 Which piece of women's gymnastic equipment is 5 metres long and 10 centimetres wide?

18 In fashion, what are jelly bean sandals or jelly shoes made from?

19 Lilith was the stern wife of which character in the American television series *Cheers*?

20 In English history, which Ws were institutions originally set up in the seventeenth century in order to provide employment for paupers?

Previous Total
1,000
800
600
450
300
200
100
50
20
0
Banked
Total

Answers

1 *Bridget Jones's Diary*	**10** Abridged
2 Coventry (City)	**11** Water
3 Julio Iglesias	**12** Blur
4 Whale (accept blue whale)	**13** A caterpillar
	14 Helmut
5 Maltese	**15** Enya
6 Proportional representation	**16** *Guys and Dolls*
	17 Balance beam/beam
7 Bill Clinton	**18** Plastic
8 Edinburgh	**19** Frasier Crane
9 72	**20** Workhouses

Round 41

1 John Piper designed the stained glass in the baptistry window in which English cathedral?

2 Which state of the USA gives its name to a black-and-yellow beetle that attacks potato crops?

3 Which pop singer sold more records in the 1990s than any other female?

4 What is the name of the grass skirt traditionally worn in Hawaii?

5 In the animal kingdom, Crabeater, Ross and Northern Fur are species of which mammal family?

6 In which country was playwright John Osborne born?

7 Which British colony, now part of China, surrendered to the Japanese on Christmas Day 1941?

8 In pop music, 'Bonehead' left which Mancunian band in 1999?

9 In what century was the electric washing machine invented?

10 During the Second World War, in which spa town was the national assembly of France based under General Pétain?

11 In sport, Sir Tom Finney played for which Lancashire soccer club throughout his entire career?

12 Boss Hogg and Daisy Duke featured in which 1970s television series?

13 The song 'I Wanna Be Like You' comes from which animated children's film?

14 In maths, 5.08 centimetres is equivalent to how many inches?

15 In the animal kingdom, a fer-de-lance is a type of which cold-blooded creature?

16 In Australia, a middy and schooner are both types of what?

17 In history, in which continent did the ancient city of Carthage stand?

18 In pop music, which Motown star began her musical career in The Primettes along with Mary Wilson, Barbara Martin and Florence Ballard?

19 In sport, by what name is toxophily better known?

20 What part of the day is a nyctophobic person afraid of?

Previous Total

1,000

800

600

450

300

200

100

50

20

0

Banked

Total

Answers

1 Coventry
2 Colorado
3 Mariah Carey
4 Hula skirt
5 Seals
6 England (accept UK)
7 Hong Kong
8 Oasis
9 Twentieth century
10 Vichy

11 Preston (North End)
12 *The Dukes of Hazzard*
13 *The Jungle Book*
14 2 inches
15 Snake
16 [Beer] glasses
17 Africa
18 Diana Ross
19 Archery
20 Night (accept dark)

Round 42

1 In literature, F. Scott Fitzgerald wrote about *The Great . . .* who?

2 In the animal kingdom, what is the opposite of 'nocturnal', meaning 'active in the daytime'?

3 In Canada, what do the letters RCMP stand for?

4 In which form of transport is a width of 1,435 millimetres known as 'standard gauge'?

5 Which country is the world's largest exporter of rice?

6 What nationality are the fashion designers Donna Karan and Calvin Klein?

7 Which John Buchan novel was adapted for the big screen in 1935, 1959 and 1978?

8 In which country did the Sharpeville Massacre take place in 1960?

9 In the UK, the River Wye flows through which two countries?

10 In politics, who was the so-called third man in the Burgess and Maclean spy case, who defected to Moscow in 1963?

11 In literature, whose science fiction works include *The First Men in the Moon*?

12 Found in milk, is lactose a sugar or an enzyme?

13 In pop music, name the female singer who released the acclaimed album *On How Life Is* in 1999.

14 Which Q is the smallest bird of the pheasant and partridge family?

15 Seville and Valencia are cities in which country?

16 In science, which metal is usually added to silver to make sterling silver: copper or zinc?

17 What is the name of the national museum and art gallery of France?

18 In children's literature, which A. A. Milne character is a bear of very little brain?

19 Which 1940s glamour icon was the star of the film *Gilda*?

20 In pop music, is Madonna's real first name 'Madonna'?

Previous Total

1,000

800

600

450

300

200

100

50

20

0

Banked

Total

Answers

1 *Gatsby*
2 Diurnal
3 Royal Canadian Mounted Police
4 Railways or trains
5 Thailand
6 American
7 *The Thirty-Nine Steps*
8 [Republic of] South Africa
9 Wales and England
10 Kim Philby
11 H. G. Wells (accept Herbert George Wells)
12 Sugar
13 Macy Gray
14 Quail
15 Spain
16 Copper
17 The Louvre
18 Winnie the Pooh (accept Pooh or Pooh Bear)
19 Rita Hayworth
20 Yes

Round 43

1 In sport, who was the last British sprinter to win the Olympic 100 metres gold medal?

2 In film, Tom Hanks and Meg Ryan were *Sleepless* in which American city?

3 In medicine, what C is a soothing ointment made from zinc carbonate?

4 Is the Canary Wharf Tower in London taller than the Eiffel Tower?

5 In sport, which Welshman was the first World Professional Darts Champion in 1978?

6 Who had a UK number one hit in 1986 with the pop song 'West End Girls'?

7 How many films are there in the Sigourney Weaver *Alien* series?

8 What letter is the chemical symbol for potassium, K or W?

9 In the New Testament, what was the name of the man who provided his own tomb for the burial of Jesus?

10 In geography, is the territory of Yukon in Mexico or Canada?

11 Complete the title of the Stevie Smith poem: 'Not Waving But . . .' what?

12 In which ocean does the island of Tahiti lie?

13 What year came before 54 BC?

14 In the animal kingdom, was 'laverock' a name used for a lark or a swan?

15 Name the mother of Michael Jackson's first bride.

16 Graphite and diamond are soft and hard examples of which chemical element?

17 The children's author Michael Bond wrote about which famous bear?

18 Isaac Asimov is best known for which kind of fiction?

19 Which basic foodstuff was rationed in July 1946 in the period of austerity following World War II?

20 The Oompa-Loompas were the small orange workers in which film starring Gene Wilder?

Previous Total

1,000

800

600

450

300

200

100

50

20

0

Banked

Total

Answers

1	Linford Christie	**15**	Priscilla Presley
2	*Seattle*	**16**	Carbon
3	Calamine	**17**	Paddington Bear
4	Yes		(accept Paddington,
5	Leighton Rees		Paddington Brown)
6	The Pet Shop Boys	**18**	Science fiction
7	Four	**19**	Bread
8	K (stands for kalium)	**20**	*Willy Wonka and the*
9	Joseph [of Arimathea]		*Chocolate Factory* (do
10	Canada		not accept *Charlie*
11	'Drowning'		*and the Chocolate*
12	Pacific		*Factory*: that was the
13	55 BC (accept 55		book)
	BCE)		
14	Lark		

Round 44

1 In computing, what does the acronym DOS stand for?

2 In television, which classic comedy series featured Captain Peacock?

3 Which *F* describes an edible, wild or domesticated, land or water bird?

4 Of which country was Valéry Giscard d'Estaing the president?

5 In which decade did the Queen open the Sydney Opera House?

6 Is the Beamish North of England Open-Air Museum in County Durham or Derbyshire?

7 Used in geometry, from which language does the letter pi (π) come?

8 In the animal kingdom, which of the following is not a freshwater fish: mackerel, pike or trout?

9 In pop music, *I've Been Expecting You* was the second UK chart-topping album from which former member of Take That?

10 What is the current UK telephone dialling code for Liverpool?

11 In which Welsh city were the 1958 British Empire and Commonwealth Games held?

12 How many moons or satellites does Mercury have?

13 In food, what name is given to lamb chops cut from the ribs nearest the leg?

14 In which European country was the film star Greta Garbo born?

15 Which Irish city is the home of the Ulster Museum?

16 In television, Arkwright and Granville were the two central characters in which BBC sitcom?

17 Which British prime minister is credited with founding the modern police force while he was home secretary?

18 In literature, which horror author wrote *Salem's Lot* and *Carrie*?

19 In which US city is Rockefeller University?

20 During which war did the British Government introduce British Summer Time?

Previous Total

1,000

800

600

450

300

200

100

50

20

0

Banked

Total

Answers

1 Disk Operating System
2 *Are You Being Served?*
3 Fowl
4 France
5 1970s (1973)
6 County Durham
7 Greek
8 Mackerel (sea fish)
9 Robbie Williams
10 0151
11 Cardiff
12 None
13 Chump chops
14 Sweden
15 Belfast
16 *Open All Hours*
17 [Sir] Robert Peel
18 Stephen King
19 New York
20 World War I (accept The Great War)

1 In astrology, in which two months could you have been born if your star sign is Taurus?

2 In sport, what was the surname of the sisters who played against each other at Wimbledon 2000?

3 Which of these cities is further from London by plane: Cape Town or Delhi?

4 In which film did Michael Caine attempt a 4-million-dollar gold-bullion heist?

5 Which city in the English Midlands has an Anglican cathedral designed by Sir Basil Spence?

6 In 1970, the voting age in Britain was lowered to 18 from what?

7 In nature, what is lacking from Australia's Nullarbor Plain?

8 What kind of steel is manufactured by adding chromium to ordinary steel?

9 In which Quentin Tarantino film did Bruce Willis play the character Butch Coolidge?

10 In sport, which American boxer was known as the Manassa Mauler?

11 On the World Wide Web, what country is represented by '.il'?

12 In history, what was the first name of the Italian soldier and patriot Garibaldi?

13 Is Zandra Rhodes a hairdresser or a fashion designer?

14 In pop music, Edele and Keavy, the twin sisters of a Boyzone member, are in which other group?

15 In literature, which author won the 1998 Booker Prize for *Amsterdam*?

16 In which decade did the hula hoop first become a popular craze?

17 Both from New Zealand, what type of animals are the kea and the kaka?

18 In education, what do the initials LEA stand for?

19 In nature, are 'garden tiger' and 'hornet clearwing' species of moths or butterflies?

20 In which British city is the National Exhibition Centre?

Previous Total

- 1,000
- 800
- 600
- 450
- 300
- 200
- 100
- 50
- 20
- 0

Banked

Total

Answers

1 April and May	**12** Giuseppe
2 Williams	**13** Fashion designer
3 Cape Town	**14** B*Witched
4 *The Italian Job*	**15** Ian McEwan
5 Coventry	**16** 1950s
6 21	**17** Birds (parrots)
7 Trees	**18** Local Education
8 Stainless	Authority
9 *Pulp Fiction*	**19** Moths
10 Jack Dempsey	**20** Birmingham
11 Israel	

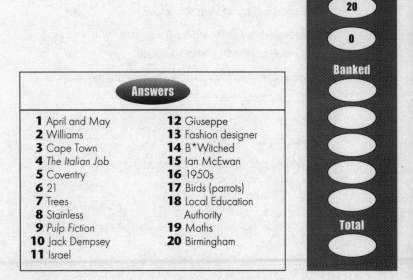

Round 46

1 In politics, Labour MP Tam Dalyell conducted a long campaign about the sinking of which Argentine ship during the Falklands war?

2 In cricket, what do the initials MCC stand for?

3 Which of these countries is largest in area: Pakistan or Mexico?

4 In a standard game of chess, how many pawns does each player have at the start of the game?

5 In science, what is measured in units called curies or rads?

6 'Old Glory' is a popular name given to the flag of which country?

7 By what acronym is the machine that picks the winning UK premium bond numbers known?

8 In food, what T is the name given to a flat bread pancake originating from Mexico?

9 'Come On You Reds' was a number one UK pop hit for which football team in 1994?

10 In astrology, the balance, or scales, is the symbol for which sign of the zodiac?

11 In literature, Ellis Peters created which medieval monk detective?

12 In the American television series, Karl Malden and Michael Douglas patrolled the streets of which US city?

13 How many days after New Year's Eve is St Valentine's Day?

14 What is the capital of Ethiopia?

15 In the animal kingdom, which Commonwealth country is the original home of the black swan?

16 The American film *Clueless*, starring Alicia Silverstone, is an adaptation of which Jane Austen novel?

17 Which English Premiership football team is nicknamed 'the Rams'?

18 In backgammon, how many pieces are there on the board in total at the start of a game?

19 Whose Little Red Book has allegedly sold over 800 million copies?

20 If a Scrabble board has fifteen rows and fifteen columns, how many squares are there on the board?

Previous Total

( )

1,000

800

600

450

300

200

100

50

20

0

Banked

Total

Answers

1 *General Belgrano* (accept *Belgrano*)	**11** Brother Cadfael
2 Marylebone Cricket Club	**12** San Francisco
	13 45 days
3 Mexico	**14** Addis Ababa
4 Eight	**15** Australia
5 Radiation (or radioactivity)	**16** *Emma*
	17 Derby [County]
6 USA	**18** 30
7 ERNIE	**19** Mao-Tse Tung (accept Chairman Mao, Mao Ze Dong)
8 Tortilla	
9 Manchester United	**20** 225
10 Libra	

Round 47

1 The film of *A Room With a View* was predominantly set in England and which other European country?

2 In physics, for what does the abbreviation UV stand?

3 Which pop song, written by Dolly Parton, was sung by Whitney Houston in the film *The Bodyguard*?

4 In classical music, how many operas did the composer Beethoven write?

5 In the children's series of books, what sort of animal is the patchwork Elmer?

6 In 1948, David Ben-Gurion became the first prime minister of which country?

7 In food, the French train pigs and dogs to hunt for which valuable underground fungus?

8 Which character in the television sitcom *Friends* is played by Lisa Kudrow?

9 'If I Were a Rich Man' is a song from which musical?

10 In sport, for which international football team does Leeds United striker Harry Kewell play?

11 In fashion, which part of a garment can be 'batwing' or 'leg of mutton'?

12 In maths, 4,840 square yards are equal to how many acres?

13 To which UK political position was Ken Livingstone elected in May 2000?

14 Which of the Queen's children has the middle names Philip, Arthur and George?

15 Which female singer has charted in the UK with the songs 'Respect' and 'I Say A Little Prayer'?

16 What is the capital of modern Egypt?

17 In literature, what nationality was the playwright Eugene O'Neill?

18 Angola and Mozambique are former colonies of which European country?

19 What was the nickname of William H. Bonney, a nineteenth-century outlaw of the American Southwest?

20 In television, Crockett and Tubbs were the central characters in which 1980s crime series?

Previous Total

1,000

800

600

450

300

200

100

50

20

0

Banked

Total

Answers

1 Italy
2 Ultraviolet
3 'I Will Always Love You'
4 One (it was *Fidelio*)
5 Elephant
6 [State of] Israel
7 Truffles
8 Phoebe
9 *Fiddler on the Roof*
10 Australia
11 Sleeve (accept arm)
12 One
13 London Mayor (accept Mayor of London; do not accept Lord Mayor of London)
14 [HRH] Prince Charles [Prince of Wales] (accept Charles)
15 Aretha Franklin
16 Cairo
17 American
18 Portugal
19 Billy the Kid
20 *Miami Vice*

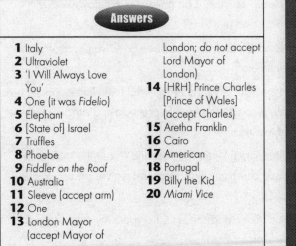

1 In astronomy, which phenomenon is composed of a nucleus, coma, head and tail?

2 From the Americas, marmosets and howlers are varieties of which animal?

3 In which Australian city would you find Bondi Beach?

4 In 1971, who declared himself president of Uganda after a coup?

5 Which semi-precious stone is made of yellowish fossil resin from trees?

6 On which Italian island is the resort town of Taormina?

7 What was Marilyn Monroe's last completed film?

8 From which country did Johan Vaaler, the man who invented the paper clip, come?

9 In drinks, which A is an Italian liqueur flavoured with apricot and almonds?

10 In sport, windsurfing has been an Olympic sport since which year?

11 On the World Wide Web, what three-letter domain code is suggested for non-profit-making organisations and institutions?

12 In the animal kingdom, hob and jill are the male and female of which domesticated creature related to the polecat?

13 The BBC comedy series *Chambers* revolves around which profession?

14 Former football manager Brian Clough was given the freedom of which city in March 1993?

15 In literature, who created Peter Pan?

16 Which former pop singer starred in the television series *Budgie*?

17 In maths, how many centimetres are there in 200 metres?

18 In sport, Trent Bridge cricket ground is in which British city?

19 In literature, who is the author of the *Goosebumps* series of children's books?

20 What does the French word *'le soleil'* translate to in English?

Previous Total

1,000
800
600
450
300
200
100
50
20
0

Banked

Total

Answers

1 A comet	**13** Legal/the law/ barristers
2 Monkeys	
3 Sydney	**14** Nottingham
4 Idi Amin (Dada)	**15** [Sir] J[ames] M[atthew] Barrie
5 Amber	
6 Sicily	**16** Adam Faith
7 *The Misfits*	**17** 20,000
8 Norway	**18** Nottingham
9 Amaretto	**19** R[obert] L[awrence] Stine
10 1984	
11 .org	**20** The sun
12 Ferret	

Round 49

1 What is the capital of the Bahamas?

2 In pop music, name the lead singer of M People, who released her solo album *Proud* in the year 2000?

3 On an Ordnance Survey map, what does 'CH' stand for?

4 In World War II, which British field marshal was nicknamed 'Monty'?

5 In education, Keele University is situated nearest which British city?

6 In literature, the title of which Joseph Heller novel has come to mean a no-win situation?

7 In sport, what nationality is the Chelsea footballer Tore Andre Flo?

8 Which international relief agency, founded by the Geneva Convention in 1864, won the Nobel Peace Prize in 1917 and 1944?

9 In Hans Christian Andersen's fairy tale *The Snow Queen*, what is the name of the little boy?

10 In pop music, name the original singer/songwriter and lead guitarist of the band Pink Floyd.

11 In fashion, what type of clothing are gauntlets, popular in the 1920s and 1930s?

12 Which film director was born Allen Stewart Konigsberg?

13 With which motor company did Austin merge in 1952?

14 What was Thomas Hardy's profession before he started writing novels?

15 Nairobi is the capital city of which African country?

16 Which order of mammals gets its name from the Latin for 'gnawing'?

17 The work of which Italian painter, born in 1884, is characterised by asymmetrical, elongated figures?

18 Which church in northern England is the largest Gothic cathedral in the UK?

19 In history, the Protestant John Knox returned from exile in 1559 to found which British Church?

20 What was the first name of Baekeland, who discovered the plastic 'Bakelite'?

Previous Total

1,000

800

600

450

300

200

100

50

20

0

Banked

Total

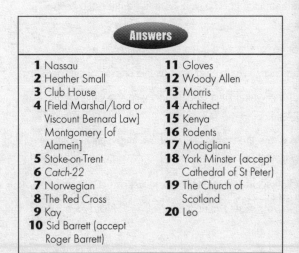

Answers

1 Nassau
2 Heather Small
3 Club House
4 [Field Marshal/Lord or Viscount Bernard Law] Montgomery [of Alamein]
5 Stoke-on-Trent
6 Catch-22
7 Norwegian
8 The Red Cross
9 Kay
10 Sid Barrett (accept Roger Barrett)
11 Gloves
12 Woody Allen
13 Morris
14 Architect
15 Kenya
16 Rodents
17 Modigliani
18 York Minster (accept Cathedral of St Peter)
19 The Church of Scotland
20 Leo

Round 50

1 Was Bram Stoker's *Dracula* published in 1697 or 1897?

2 'I Don't Know How To Love Him' is a song from which Andrew Lloyd Webber musical?

3 Does the Great Barrier Reef lie off the north-eastern or north-western coast of Australia?

4 In classical music, was Erroll Garner famed for playing the piano or the cello?

5 In geography, which of these countries is the largest in area: Libya or Liberia?

6 In clothing, which *B* is the name for the circular straw hat with a flat top and straight brim?

7 Which actor played Dr Frank Bryant in the 1983 film *Educating Rita*?

8 Is the tympanic membrane located in the nose or the ear?

9 In nature, are spruce trees deciduous or evergreen?

10 In chemistry, which element has the chemical symbol O_2?

11 In history, which king of England was the illegitimate son of Duke Robert the Devil?

12 Who wrote the ballet *The Firebird*, Stravinsky or Schubert?

13 In which sport is a pommel horse used?

14 Which tree shares its name with Oliver Hardy's partner?

15 Is it true or false that new electric blankets normally come fitted with a 13-amp fuse?

16 Who played Oskar Schindler in the 1993 film *Schindler's List*?

17 In which Utah city might you visit the Beehive House and the Mormon Tabernacle?

18 In Britain, in which year did it become compulsory for cars to have registration plates: 1904 or 1911?

19 What is the normal meaning of the cockney rhyming slang 'apples and pears'?

20 In TV, name the scientist played by Bill Bixby who turned into the Incredible Hulk when angry?

Previous Total

1,000

800

600

450

300

200

100

50

20

0

Banked

Total

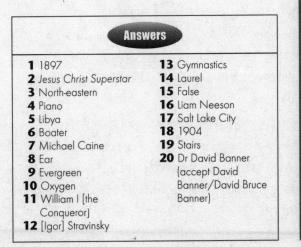

Answers

1 1897
2 *Jesus Christ Superstar*
3 North-eastern
4 Piano
5 Libya
6 Boater
7 Michael Caine
8 Ear
9 Evergreen
10 Oxygen
11 William I [the Conqueror]
12 [Igor] Stravinsky

13 Gymnastics
14 Laurel
15 False
16 Liam Neeson
17 Salt Lake City
18 1904
19 Stairs
20 Dr David Banner (accept David Banner/David Bruce Banner)

Round 51

1 Is Australia ahead of or behind GMT?

2 In which American city might you take a tour of television's South Fork Ranch?

3 In literature, in which century did the American poet Emily Dickinson write?

4 If you travelled direct by train from Ipswich to London, at which London terminus would you arrive?

5 In the animal kingdom, which of Santa's reindeer shares its name with the word for a female fox?

6 Which of Pierce Brosnan's James Bond movies shares its name with a type of duck?

7 Is it true or false that Madrid's underground railway is called 'the Metro'?

8 In food, jasmine, sticky and long-grain are all types of what?

9 In the novel *Nicholas Nickleby* by Charles Dickens, does the character Nicholas ever actually appear?

10 In 1966, which music star recorded the album *Blonde on Blonde*?

11 In which century did the Suez Canal open?

12 In the animal kingdom, 'ringlet' and 'purple hairstreak' are both types of which insect?

13 In the human body, are the temporal bones in the foot or the head?

14 In science, which element's name comes from the Latin for 'charcoal', and has the symbol C?

15 What were the first names of the two Kellys who presented the television series *Game For A Laugh*?

16 The holder of which political post is the chief law officer of the crown in England and Wales?

17 In World War II, which country erected the Metaxas Line facing Bulgaria: Greece or Yugoslavia?

18 In which Yorkshire town might you cross The Stray to reach The Valley Gardens?

19 Is an angstrom a unit of measure for very small or very large distances?

20 Is it true to say that those afflicted with Daltonism are colour blind?

Previous Total

1,000
800
600
450
300
200
100
50
20
0

Banked

Total

Answers

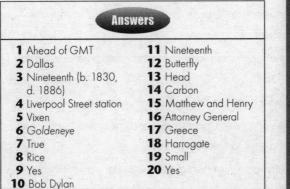

1 Ahead of GMT	**11** Nineteenth
2 Dallas	**12** Butterfly
3 Nineteenth (b. 1830, d. 1886)	**13** Head
	14 Carbon
4 Liverpool Street station	**15** Matthew and Henry
5 Vixen	**16** Attorney General
6 *Goldeneye*	**17** Greece
7 True	**18** Harrogate
8 Rice	**19** Small
9 Yes	**20** Yes
10 Bob Dylan	

Round 52

1 On 4 July 1997, an American *Pathfinder* spacecraft landed on which planet?

2 In medicine, digitoxin and digitalis are derived from which flowering plant?

3 In the eighteenth century, John Wesley founded the movement which became the Methodist Church. What was the name of his famous hymn-writing brother?

4 *A Close Shave* was the third film in which Oscar-winning film series by Nick Park?

5 In biology, in which organ of the body is the retina?

6 Which G is the mineral from which plaster of Paris is made?

7 What is the name of the BBC's comedy fund-raising event which takes place on Red Nose Day?

8 Did *The Beano* comic first appear in the 1930s or the 1960s?

9 In music, is a 'ligature' part of the French horn or the clarinet?

10 In the UK, where would you be if the postcode began with G?

11 In food, Cornish Yarg is a type of what?

12 In history, which English monarch decided to dissolve Parliament for eleven years?

13 Which ballerina and actress was the star of the film *The Red Shoes*?

14 Which C is the term for the mandatory requirement to enlist in the military?

15 In the nursery rhyme, what was Miss Muffet eating?

16 In which South American city is the statue of Christ the Redeemer found?

17 Which Alfred Hitchcock film contains a notorious shower scene?

18 Between which two countries was the first Opium War fought in the nineteenth century?

19 In US politics, when JFK was killed, was he the seventh or the eighth American president to have died in office?

20 In astrology, which star sign falls between the star signs of Scorpio and Capricorn?

Previous Total

1,000

800

600

450

300

200

100

50

20

0

Banked

Total

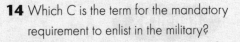

Answers

1 Mars	**12** Charles I
2 Foxglove	**13** Moira Shearer
3 Charles Wesley	**14** Conscription
4 *Wallace and Gromit*	**15** Curds and whey
5 Eye	**16** Rio de Janeiro
6 Gypsum	**17** *Psycho*
7 Comic Relief	**18** China and Britain
8 1930s	**19** Eighth
9 Clarinet	**20** Sagittarius
10 Glasgow	
11 Cheese	

Round 53

1 In darts, does the outer ring or the inner ring represent a double score?

2 What is the Spanish word for the number two?

3 In which period did the first birds appear: Jurassic or Cretaceous?

4 Which 1980s television show was set in the New York City High School for the Performing Arts?

5 In meteorology, what *A* describes a large system of wind rotating about an area of high atmospheric pressure?

6 In pop music, what colour eyes did Van Morrison's girl have in his classic song?

7 In football, with which international team would you associate the goalkeeper Pat Jennings?

8 Does the song 'Bali Ha'i' come from the musical *South Pacific* or *Brigadoon*?

9 Is the medical term for the windpipe the cochlea or the trachea?

10 In fashion, the bolero is a short jacket originally from which country?

11 In film, who won an Oscar for her portrayal of Fanny Brice in *Funny Girl*?

12 How did the author Sir James Matthew Barrie, born in 1860, style his name on his books?

13 The Englishman Ernest Swinton prompted the invention of which military vehicle in 1914?

14 In the animal kingdom, which part of a hare is known as its 'scut'?

15 In 1958, which fuel became the last commodity to be de-rationed in the period of austerity following World War II?

16 In which English city might you walk from St George's Hall to Lime St Station?

17 What is the name of Frank Sinatra's singing daughter?

18 In open court, how should one correctly address a county court judge?

19 In science, which gas, discovered in 1898, was given a name meaning 'new' in Greek?

20 In French politics, who first became prime minister in 1974?

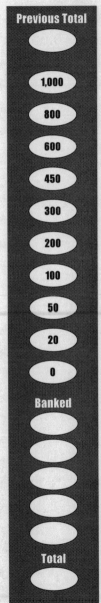

Previous Total

1,000

800

600

450

300

200

100

50

20

0

Banked

Total

Answers

1 The outer ring	**11** Barbra Streisand
2 *Dos*	**12** J. M. Barrie
3 Jurassic	**13** Tank (accept His
4 *Fame*	Majesty's Land Ship)
5 Anticyclone	**14** Tail
6 Brown	**15** Coal
7 Northern Ireland	**16** Liverpool
(accept Ulster)	**17** Nancy Sinatra
8 *South Pacific*	**18** 'Your Honour'
9 Trachea	**19** Neon
10 Spain	**20** Jacques Chirac

1 In the cable of a modern electric kettle, what colour is the neutral wire?

2 In which US city might you visit Bourbon Street and Basin Street?

3 In astrology, name one of the months you could have been born in if your star sign is Cancer.

4 Which long-running television programme showed sheepdog championship trials?

5 In geography, on which island might you visit Nelson's Statue in Trafalgar Square, Bridgetown?

6 *Mus musculus* is the Latin name for which household pest?

7 What popular French sandwich has a name that literally means either 'crunch sir' or 'munch sir'?

8 Which actress and singer played Billie Holliday in the 1972 film *Lady Sings the Blues*?

9 In television, which former *Blue Peter* presenter went on to become a darts presenter?

10 In the animal kingdom, what kind of creature is a 'Moorish idol'?

11 In literature, what was the first name of Boswell, the famed biographer of Samuel Johnson?

12 In politics, who was prime minister of the Irish Republic from 1992 to 1994?

13 In pop music, which Welshman was discovered singing under the name of Tommy Scott in 1964?

14 In the animal kingdom, does a bee have ears?

15 In maths, how many prime numbers are there between 15 and 20?

16 Who played the title role in the television comedy series *Chef!*?

17 Which Victorian novelist wrote *Barnaby Rudge*, first published in serial form in 1841?

18 Who starred in and directed the 1977 Academy Award-winning film *Annie Hall*?

19 The author Reverend W. V. Awdrey wrote children's books about which famous blue engine?

20 General Manuel Noriega was the ruler of which Central American country until an invasion by the United States in 1989?

Previous Total

1,000
800
600
450
300
200
100
50
20
0

Banked

Total

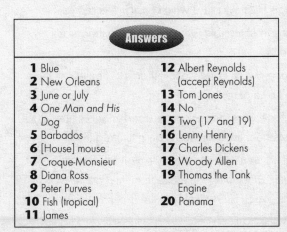

Answers

1 Blue
2 New Orleans
3 June or July
4 *One Man and His Dog*
5 Barbados
6 [House] mouse
7 Croque-Monsieur
8 Diana Ross
9 Peter Purves
10 Fish (tropical)
11 James
12 Albert Reynolds (accept Reynolds)
13 Tom Jones
14 No
15 Two (17 and 19)
16 Lenny Henry
17 Charles Dickens
18 Woody Allen
19 Thomas the Tank Engine
20 Panama

Round 55

1 Which American composer wrote *An American in Paris* in 1928?

2 The fashion designer Alexander McQueen comes from which English city?

3 In the UK, what is traditionally given as a present on the 50th wedding anniversary?

4 Which actress played the role of Angela McCourt in the 1999 film *Angela's Ashes*?

5 Apiphobia is a fear of which insects?

6 What is the UK telephone dialling code for Edinburgh?

7 Which food writer and journalist wrote the book *How To Eat: the pleasure and principles of good food*?

8 In which US city might you visit The Cannery and Golden Gate Bridge?

9 In television, the actor who played Tucker Jenkins in *Grange Hill* now plays which *EastEnders* regular?

10 What sort of triangle is the subject of Pythagoras' theorem?

11 In space, which constellation shares its name with the flying horse of mythology?

12 Which debating society announced in September 2000 that Michael Jackson would be a future guest?

13 What name is given to the collection of Greek sculptures, including the frieze from the Parthenon in Athens, which is on display in the British Museum?

14 In which Canadian city might you visit Yorkville and the Ontario Science Centre?

15 Which British playwright, famous for his dramatic pause, wrote *The Homecoming*, published and performed in 1965?

16 In nature, what is the more common name for nacre, which lines the shell of an oyster?

17 Which British band recorded the albums *A Night at the Opera* and *A Day at the Races*?

18 Which actor played boxer Rubin 'Hurricane' Carter in the 1999 film *The Hurricane*?

19 In history, which castle in Saxony was used to house prisoners likely to escape during the Second World War?

20 Bottled milk from Jersey and Guernsey cows has a foil cap of what colour?

Previous Total

( )
(1,000)
(800)
(600)
(450)
(300)
(200)
(100)
(50)
(20)
(0)

Banked

( )
( )
( )
( )
( )

Total

( )

Answers

1 George Gershwin	**13** The Elgin Marbles
2 London	**14** Toronto
3 Gold	**15** [Harold] Pinter
4 Emily Watson	**16** Mother-of-pearl
5 Bees	**17** Queen
6 0131	**18** Denzel Washington
7 Nigella Lawson	**19** Colditz
8 San Francisco	**20** Gold
9 Mark Fowler	
10 Right-angled triangle	
11 Pegasus	
12 Oxford Union (if answer is Oxford or Oxford University, ask to be more specific)	

Round 56

1 What sort of clock was the 'clepsydra', used by the Romans?

2 To which English football club was Paul Gascoigne under contract between 1988 and 1992?

3 According to the nursery rhyme, what is Monday's child?

4 In literature, what is the title of Helen Fielding's second Bridget Jones novel?

5 Ray Davies was the lead singer of which British pop group?

6 If the letter A is denoted by the number 1 and B by the number 2, which word is denoted by the numbers 1-3-5?

7 What word can mean a round loaf of bread, a small horse or a male swan?

8 In medical science, pathology is the study of the causes and effects of what?

9 Which country does the music group Kraftwerk come from?

10 Which actor played Larry in the 1999 film *The Big Kahuna*?

11 'Shar Pei' and 'Rhodesian ridgeback' are both breeds of which animal?

12 Prior to the reunification of Germany, what was the capital of West Germany?

13 Which football team had a UK Top 10 chart hit in 1988 with 'Anfield Rap'?

14 On which island might you visit the Tuff Gong Studio, with its museum to Bob Marley?

15 Port Said and Rosetta are in which country?

16 The wreck of which German World War II battleship was located on the sea bottom in June 1989?

17 From which Latin American country did the twentieth-century artist Frida Kahlo come?

18 Which female poet wrote *The Bell Jar*, first published in 1963 under the pseudonym Victoria Lucas?

19 What was the nationality of 1960s gymnastics star Vera Caslavska?

20 In film, which actor played Jake La Motta in the 1980 film *Raging Bull*?

Previous Total

1,000

800

600

450

300

200

100

50

20

0

Banked

Total

Answers

1 Water clock
2 Tottenham Hotspur (accept Spurs)
3 Fair of face
4 [*Bridget Jones:*] *The Edge of Reason*
5 The Kinks
6 Ace
7 Cob
8 Disease (accept [causes of] death)
9 Germany
10 Kevin Spacey
11 Dog
12 Bonn
13 Liverpool
14 Jamaica
15 Egypt
16 *Bismarck*
17 Mexico
18 Sylvia Plath
19 Czech
20 Robert De Niro

Round 57

1 The songs 'Sweet Dreams Are Made of This' and 'Miracle of Love' were released by which pop band?

2 Korean industrialist Sun Myung Moon founded which religious movement in 1954?

3 Which ancient Greek poet shares his name with a character in the cartoon The Simpsons?

4 In history, shoguns were the military dictators of which country until 1867?

5 In medicine, what term is used to describe an inherited disease characterised by the inability of the blood to clot?

6 In television's Star Trek, which starship captain is associated with the phrase 'Beam me up, Scotty'?

7 Which Impressionist artist famously painted different versions of the façade of Rouen Cathedral in the 1890s?

8 Which seventeenth-century English poet wrote the epic poem Paradise Lost?

9 From which country did Brazil declare independence in 1822?

10 In boxing, who did Muhammad Ali defeat in Zaire in the 1974 fight dubbed 'the rumble in the jungle'?

11 Which Scottish football team plays at Ibrox stadium?

12 In television, which flamboyant Dame is known for saying 'Hello possums'?

13 In Greek mythology, which king of Phrygia was granted the gift of converting everything he touched to gold?

14 In Hans Christian Andersen's tale, the Ugly Duckling grew into which fine bird?

15 In the animal kingdom, is the 'okapi' a relative of the zebra or the giraffe?

16 In pop music, what group's singles include 'You Really Got Me' and 'Waterloo Sunset'?

17 Which now-extinct creature looked like an elephant with a thick coat of hair?

18 In cockney rhyming slang, which piece of furniture is a 'Cain and Abel'?

19 Which Mediterranean principality is the home of the Monte Carlo Casino?

20 In what decade did Nancy, Lady Astor become the first woman to take her seat in the House of Commons?

Previous Total

( )

1,000

800

600

450

300

200

100

50

20

0

Banked

( )
( )
( )
( )
( )

Total

( )

Answers

1 Eurythmics
2 Unification Church (accept Moonies or Holy Spirit Association for the Unification of World Christianity)
3 Homer
4 Japan
5 Haemophilia
6 Captain Kirk
7 Monet
8 John Milton
9 Portugal
10 George Foreman
11 [Glasgow] Rangers
12 Dame Edna Everage (accept Edna Everage; do not accept Barry Humphreys)
13 Midas
14 Swan
15 Giraffe
16 The Kinks
17 Mammoth (accept mastodon)
18 Table
19 Monaco
20 1910s (1919)

Round 58

1 In which British town might you visit the Golden Mile and the Tower Ballroom?

2 In nature, what G describes long, airborne lines of spider silk?

3 Which nation formally surrendered to the Americans on the battleship USS *Missouri* on 2 September 1945?

4 In film, who won an Oscar for his performance in *The King and I*?

5 What is the UK telephone dialling code for Glasgow?

6 In science, which element has the chemical symbol Ag?

7 Which B was a famous 1960s London fashion store opened by Barbara Hulanski?

8 Is it true that haemophilia is a disease mainly suffered by men?

9 In UK politics, which Conservative became MP for Henley in 1974?

10 Is myrtle a species of bird or a species of plant?

11 In which ocean do the Seychelles lie?

12 Is endocrinology the study of nerves or hormones?

13 In classical music, what B is a Spanish dance in moderate triple time?

14 In transport, which is the only London mainline rail terminus to share its name with a bridge over the Thames?

15 In which televised sport did Giant Haystacks become a household name?

16 In literature, what is the surname of Ogden, an American writer of elaborate light verse?

17 In maths, how many prime numbers are there between 10 and 15?

18 Which actress played the spurned lover in the 1987 film *Fatal Attraction*?

19 Which Irish presenter fronted the BBC television quiz show *Going For Gold*?

20 In the proverb, where does charity begin?

Previous Total

1,000
800
600
450
300
200
100
50
20
0

Banked

Total

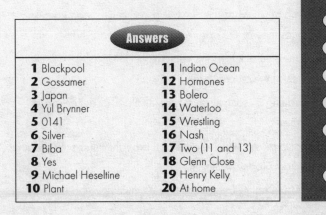

Answers

1 Blackpool	**11** Indian Ocean
2 Gossamer	**12** Hormones
3 Japan	**13** Bolero
4 Yul Brynner	**14** Waterloo
5 0141	**15** Wrestling
6 Silver	**16** Nash
7 Biba	**17** Two (11 and 13)
8 Yes	**18** Glenn Close
9 Michael Heseltine	**19** Henry Kelly
10 Plant	**20** At home

Round 59

1 In art, did Christopher Nevinson paint images of the First World War or the Second World War?

2 If the registration plate on a Spanish vehicle shows the letter B, what city does it come from?

3 Is gluteus maximus the name of a Roman emperor or a muscle in the body?

4 Who has a political breakfast on BBC1 on Sunday morning?

5 Was Dartmoor or Exmoor the first to be designated as a National Park?

6 Who was the first president of the United States of America to serve two terms?

7 What was the first name of Captain Webb, the first man to swim the English Channel?

8 In history, was income tax introduced in 1799 by a Tory or a Whig prime minister?

9 In maths, at what speed would you have been travelling if a journey of 60 miles took an hour and a half?

10 In the animal kingdom, vampire and horseshoe are both types of which creature?

11 In nature, is 'spirogyra' a type of black insect or green algae?

12 In pop music, which Spice Girl brought out a solo album entitled *Northern Star*?

13 Is it true that in Gibraltar vehicles must drive on the left?

14 Which two countries jointly hosted the Euro 2000 football championships?

15 'I wandered lonely as a cloud' is the first line of a poem written in 1804 by whom?

16 In the USA, Fremont Street and The Strip are features of which gambler's paradise?

17 In nature, which insect's nest is called a 'formicary'?

18 Which French actor, born in 1948, starred in the 1990 movie *Cyrano de Bergerac*?

19 In human biology, does the pleura membrane cover the liver or the lungs?

20 During the sixteenth century, the artist Tintoretto flourished in which Italian city?

Previous Total

1,000
800
600
450
300
200
100
50
20
0

Banked

Total

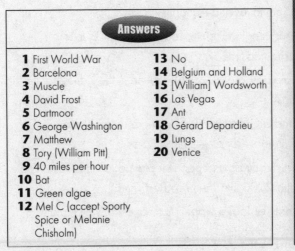

Answers

1 First World War
2 Barcelona
3 Muscle
4 David Frost
5 Dartmoor
6 George Washington
7 Matthew
8 Tory (William Pitt)
9 40 miles per hour
10 Bat
11 Green algae
12 Mel C (accept Sporty Spice or Melanie Chisholm)
13 No
14 Belgium and Holland
15 [William] Wordsworth
16 Las Vegas
17 Ant
18 Gérard Depardieu
19 Lungs
20 Venice

Round 60

1 Which stately home of North Yorkshire was the main setting for the television dramatisation of *Brideshead Revisited*?

2 In astronomy, does a planet or a comet have a name meaning 'wanderer' in Greek?

3 In literature, poet Philip Larkin was born in which century?

4 In the animal kingdom, is a hare's 'form', or lair, above the ground or below the ground?

5 What nationality is the monetarist economist Milton Friedman?

6 From which political party was Liverpudlian Derek Hatton expelled in 1987?

7 In astrology, which star sign falls between the star signs of Sagittarius and Aquarius?

8 Which English Premier League football club is nicknamed 'The Magpies'?

9 In biology, are bronchioles found in the kidneys or the lungs?

10 In the UK, in which decade were L-plates made compulsory for all learner drivers?

11 Which actress and pop star played the character Abbie in the 2000 film *The Next Best Thing*?

12 In nature, 'lady's slipper' is a variety of which plant, a rose or an orchid?

13 In the animal kingdom, how many legs does a cobweb spider have?

14 In English, of which phrase is ASAP an abbreviation?

15 'Cubic zirconia' is sold as a popular substitute for which stone?

16 Penny and Vince were ill-fated lovers in which television comedy series?

17 In the cable of a modern electric toaster, what colour is the live wire?

18 Which English punk band released the album *London Calling* in 1979?

19 In sport, Martin O'Neill left Leicester City to become the manager of which Scottish football club?

20 In chemistry, what substance is produced by burning hydrogen in air?

Previous Total

1,000

800

600

450

300

200

100

50

20

0

Banked

Total

Answers

1 Castle Howard
2 Planet
3 Twentieth century (1922)
4 Above ground
5 American
6 Labour
7 Capricorn
8 Newcastle United
9 Lungs
10 1930s (1935)

11 Madonna
12 Orchid
13 Eight
14 As soon as possible
15 Diamond
16 *Just Good Friends*
17 Brown
18 The Clash
19 [Glasgow] Celtic
20 Water

Round 61

1 In which decade did Wallace Carothers develop nylon?

2 'Tod' is a dialect word for which predatory mammal?

3 In history, which British-born statesman formed the British South Africa Company in 1889?

4 If A is Alpha and Z is Zulu, what is Y?

5 Limahl was the lead singer of which 1980s pop group?

6 In the UK, traditionally, the violet is a flower associated with which month?

7 Which European capital fell to the Germans on 27 September 1939, nearly four weeks after Poland was invaded?

8 For which country did Viv Richards play test cricket?

9 In which Egyptian city might you visit the Citadel and Ramses Square?

10 In politics, who became International Development Secretary after Labour's 1997 general election victory?

11 In physics, what is measured in lamberts or lumens?

12 Fisherman's Wharf and Nob Hill are landmarks of which Californian city?

13 Who was the first American president to shake hands with Cuban leader Fidel Castro?

14 The resort of Torremolinos is on which of the Spanish 'Costas'?

15 In astrology, name one of the two months you could have been born in if your star sign is Virgo.

16 In literature, which poet wrote 'Ode to a Nightingale' in 1819?

17 If the speedometer on your car says you are travelling at 120 kilometres per hour, how fast are you going in miles per hour?

18 Who played the female lead in the BBC television drama *The Sculptress*?

19 In geography, Dunn's River Falls at Ocho Rios is a feature of which island?

20 In the animal kingdom, Sika and fallow are both types of which animal?

Previous Total

1,000
800
600
450
300
200
100
50
20
0

Banked

Total

Answers

1 1930s (1934)
2 Fox
3 Cecil Rhodes
4 Yankee
5 Kajagoogoo
6 February
7 Warsaw
8 West Indies
9 Cairo
10 Clare Short
11 Light, or brightness (accept luminosity)
12 San Francisco
13 Bill Clinton (accept also President [William Jefferson] Clinton)
14 Costa del Sol
15 August or September
16 [John] Keats
17 75 mph
18 Pauline Quirke
19 Jamaica
20 Deer

Round 62

1 Russian president Vladimir Putin is an accomplished exponent of which martial art?

2 In nature, 'durmast', 'common' and 'turkey' are all types of which tree found in Britain?

3 Which rock star presented a petition against third-world debt at the UN Millennium Summit in September 2000?

4 In farming, which C is a machine used to separate the wheat from the chaff?

5 What year comes before 99 BC?

6 In which village were the antics of *Noel's House Party* said to take place?

7 Which style of English architecture takes its name from the reign of James I?

8 The title character in the 1996 film *Happy Gilmore* becomes a champion in which sport?

9 Duncan was the king of Scotland in which Shakespeare play?

10 What is the surname of the brothers in the pop group The Bee Gees?

11 In the Beatrix Potter story, what is the name of Flopsy, Mopsy and Cotton-tail's brother?

12 Which of these cities is furthest from London by plane: Warsaw or Casablanca?

13 In history, which country fought alongside France against Nelson's British fleet at the Battle of Trafalgar?

14 Who did Lisa Marie Presley marry in the Dominican Republic on 26 May 1994?

15 In the animal kingdom, how many claws does a golden eagle have on each foot?

16 In television, Wendy Richard and Bill Treacher played which *EastEnders* couple?

17 In classical music, who composed the Overture to *A Midsummer Night's Dream* in the late 1820s?

18 For which English Premiership football team does Paul Scholes play?

19 In fashion, what is a 'homburg'?

20 In history, in which Punjabi city did a massacre of Sikhs by British troops take place in 1919?

Previous Total

1,000

800

600

450

300

200

100

50

20

0

Banked

Total

Answers

1 Judo
2 Oak
3 Bono
4 Combine harvester
5 100 BC (accept 100 BCE)
6 Crinkly Bottom
7 Jacobean
8 Golf
9 *Macbeth*
10 Gibb
11 Peter Rabbit (accept Peter)
12 Casablanca
13 Spain
14 Michael Jackson
15 Four
16 Pauline and Arthur Fowler
17 [Felix] Mendelssohn (accept Jacob Ludwig Felix Mendelssohn-Bartholdy)
18 Manchester United
19 A hat
20 Amritsar

Round 63

1 From whom did Sue Barker take over as the host of the television programme *A Question of Sport*?

2 The tourist attractions of which US city include the Peabody Hotel and Graceland?

3 In maths, if a runner in a mile race has completed three-quarters of the course, how many more yards has he got left to run?

4 What was the name of the man-eating plant in *Little Shop of Horrors*?

5 What is the first name of the famous designer Armani?

6 Which body in our solar system has a diameter of 865,000 miles?

7 In the animal kingdom, what colour is the rat whose latin name is *Rattus rattus*?

8 In which Canadian city might you glimpse Niagara from the CN Tower?

9 In pop music, what is the home town of the boy band Boyzone?

10 According to Norse legend, which bird delivers new-born babies to the home?

11 Who directed the 1999 film *The Talented Mr Ripley*?

12 In history, the name of which city in Nebraska was used as the codename of one of the beaches used in the Normandy landings on D-Day?

13 In which decade did Sir Alec Jeffreys discover DNA profiling?

14 In which US city might you visit Carnegie Hall and Central Park?

15 In law, what C is the name for the person to whom a debt is owed?

16 In nature, what sort of bird is a Red-breasted Merganser?

17 In which food-based television detective series would you find the character Henry Crabbe?

18 Which form of calcium carbonate did Michelangelo use for his statue *David*?

19 Which country were beaten by a 'golden goal' in the final of football's Euro 2000 championships?

20 In the nursery rhyme about Jack and Jill, which of the two fell down and broke their crown?

Previous Total

( )

(1,000)

(800)

(600)

(450)

(300)

(200)

(100)

(50)

(20)

(0)

Banked

Total

Answers

1 David Coleman	**11** Anthony Minghella
2 Memphis	**12** Omaha
3 440 yards	**13** 1980s
4 Audrey Two (do not accept Audrey)	**14** New York
5 Giorgio	**15** Creditor
6 The sun	**16** Duck
7 Black	**17** *Pie in the Sky*
8 Toronto	**18** Marble
9 Dublin	**19** Italy
10 Stork	**20** Jack

Round 64

1 The Rows and the Roodee Racecourse are landmarks of which British city?

2 Which word can mean both a college and a group of whales?

3 On the internet, what does IP stand for?

4 Despite its name, the slow-worm is really a type of which reptile?

5 Which Hollywood film star performed in a pop band called The Bacon Brothers?

6 In which men's gymnastics event are two wires suspended over 5 metres from the floor?

7 The television quiz show *Bob's Full House* was based on which game?

8 On which island might you visit Sam Lord's Castle and Bridgetown's Careenage?

9 Of which country is Bucharest the capital?

10 What sort of rats were the British 7th Armoured Division, according to their nickname during the Second World War?

11 In art, Monet painted a series of canvases on the banks of the river Epte that featured which trees?

12 Which English poet of the sixteenth century wrote the *Arcadia*?

13 Established by the United Nations in 1946, which global organisation aims to eradicate preventable diseases?

14 In fashion, name either of the garments which make up a twin set.

15 Cheviot and Romney are breeds of which farm animal?

16 Which US city is Benjamin Franklin's birthplace and the venue of a famous 1773 Tea Party?

17 Of which country is the volcanic island Krakatoa a part?

18 In literature, who is the hero of the novel *The Thirty-Nine Steps* by John Buchan?

19 In food, with which fruit is a fish dish described as 'Véronique' garnished?

20 Which cartoon family lived at 345 Stonecave Road, Bedrock?

Previous Total

1,000

800

600

450

300

200

100

50

20

0

Banked

Total

Answers

1 Chester
2 School
3 Internet protocol
4 Lizard
5 Kevin Bacon
6 Rings (accept stationary rings)
7 Bingo
8 Barbados
9 Romania
10 Desert Rats
11 Poplar trees
12 [Sir Philip] Sidney
13 World Health Organization
14 Cardigan or jumper (accept tank top, sweater)
15 Sheep
16 Boston
17 Indonesia
18 [Brigadier-General Sir] Richard Hannay (accept Dick Hannay)
19 [White] grapes
20 The Flintstones

Round 65

1 Who was British prime minister when the country joined the European Economic Community in 1973?

2 Which usually fatal disease of pigs is also known as 'hog cholera'?

3 In food, which root crop was originally known as the 'Swedish turnip'?

4 In which decade was the pocket calculator invented?

5 Who is Debbie Reynolds's famous actress daughter?

6 In the human body, what happens to the rate of the heart beat during exercise?

7 In which decade was the broadcaster Terry Wogan born?

8 Who led the Romanian Communist Party from 1965 until his execution in 1989?

9 What colour is the caravan symbol on an Ordnance Survey map?

10 In physics, what P is a triangular block of glass that splits a beam of white light into colours of the spectrum?

11 How many times was Marilyn Monroe nominated for an Academy Award?

12 In pop music, complete the title of this UK Blondie hit: 'Heart of . . .'?

13 In literature, which Charles Dickens novel has a central character known as Pip?

14 Traditionally, is red or white wine used in the French dish coq *au vin*?

15 In nature, what C is the embryo stage of a butterfly's life-cycle?

16 In fashion, was the 'farthingale' worn in the Elizabethan or Georgian period?

17 In pop music, which American record label was founded by Berry Gordy?

18 In the animal kingdom, what is a female swan called?

19 In which century was the teabag invented?

20 How many symphonies did the composer Tchaikovsky complete during his lifetime: six or eight?

Previous Total

◯

1,000

800

600

450

300

200

100

50

20

0

Banked

◯

◯

◯

◯

◯

Total

◯

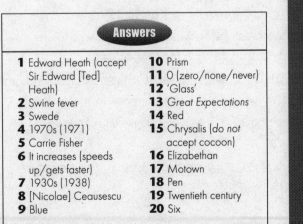

Answers

1 Edward Heath (accept Sir Edward [Ted] Heath)
2 Swine fever
3 Swede
4 1970s (1971)
5 Carrie Fisher
6 It increases (speeds up/gets faster)
7 1930s (1938)
8 [Nicolae] Ceausescu
9 Blue
10 Prism
11 0 (zero/none/never)
12 'Glass'
13 *Great Expectations*
14 Red
15 Chrysalis (do not accept cocoon)
16 Elizabethan
17 Motown
18 Pen
19 Twentieth century
20 Six

Round 66

1 Which female scientist discovered polonium, naming it after her native Poland?

2 In history, who assumed the title 'Führer of Germany' after the death of President von Hindenburg in 1934?

3 In the UK, A-road signs have a green background. What colour background is used for signs to tourist attractions?

4 What is the current UK telephone dialling code for Nottingham?

5 In literature, does an epistolary novel refer to a novel made up of correspondence or a novel written by a child?

6 In Greek architecture, is an 'entablature' above or below a column?

7 Which city in China is the largest in area?

8 In food, does the Adzuki bean originate in Asia or Central America?

9 Which country did the rock group INXS come from?

10 Viscount Alanbrooke was chief of the British Imperial General Staff during which World War?

11 Which Q is a drug obtained from the bark of the cinchona tree, which was once commonly used to treat malaria?

12 Was Elgar's First Symphony premiered in Manchester or London?

13 What part of the human body makes up the majority of household dust?

14 What was the first name of Birdseye, the inventor of commercial frozen food processing?

15 In which UK television soap might the characters drink at The Queen Vic?

16 In geography, the city of Bristol stands on which river?

17 In geometry, πr^2 ('pi R squared') is the formula to determine the area of which shape?

18 On land, a group of which birds is called a 'gaggle'?

19 In history, Sir John Joseph Caldwell Abbott served as prime minister of which country from 1891 to 1892: Canada or the USA?

20 When a boat is sailing 'close-hauled' is the wind blowing from ahead, behind, or from the side?

Previous Total

1,000

800

600

450

300

200

100

50

20

0

Banked

Total

Answers

1 Marie Curie (accept Manya Sklodowska)
2 Adolf Hitler
3 Brown
4 0115
5 Made up of correspondence
6 Above
7 Shanghai
8 Asia
9 Australia
10 World War II
11 Quinine
12 Manchester
13 Dead skin cells/skin
14 Clarence
15 *EastEnders*
16 Avon
17 Circle
18 Geese
19 Canada
20 Ahead

Round 67

1 Which A is a respiratory condition, leading to constriction of the bronchioles, which can trigger coughing, breathlessness and wheezing?

2 In architecture, is the Early English style considered to be Gothic or baroque?

3 In the television programme *The Lone Ranger*, what was the name of Tonto's horse?

4 At a ranch owned by which pop star did Elizabeth Taylor marry Larry Fortensky in 1991?

5 In classical music, who composed *La Bohème*: Puccini or Bizet?

6 What is the capital of the Isle of Man?

7 In food, a Wiener schnitzel traditionally consists of a cutlet of which meat coated with breadcrumbs and fried?

8 In medicine, is the disease tuberculosis contagious?

9 The first Boer War in South Africa took place during the reign of which British monarch?

10 Which Shakespeare play features Banquo, who is told by witches that his sons will be kings?

11 In the animal kingdom, from which continent does the orang-utan come?

12 In the nursery rhyme beginning 'Hey diddle diddle', which animal 'laughed to see such sport'?

13 Following attacks on German dams in World War II, the RAF 617 Squadron acquired which nickname?

14 In astrology, the star sign Scorpio is represented by which creature?

15 In Rugby Union, the player in which position usually carries the number 15?

16 In theatre, were the playwrights William Congreve and William Wycherley English or American?

17 If A is Alpha and Z is Zulu, what is C?

18 Complete the title of this James Bond film: *Live and . . .* what?

19 Which London public building was the first to be lit by electric lighting?

20 In chemistry, what is the literal English translation of 'aqua fortis', the Latin name for nitric acid?

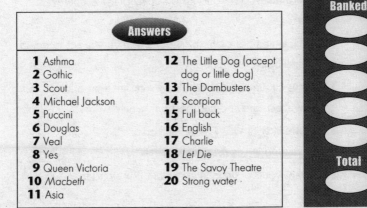

Previous Total

1,000
800
600
450
300
200
100
50
20
0

Banked

Total

Answers

1 Asthma	**12** The Little Dog (accept dog or little dog)
2 Gothic	**13** The Dambusters
3 Scout	**14** Scorpion
4 Michael Jackson	**15** Full back
5 Puccini	**16** English
6 Douglas	**17** Charlie
7 Veal	**18** *Let Die*
8 Yes	**19** The Savoy Theatre
9 Queen Victoria	**20** Strong water ·
10 *Macbeth*	
11 Asia	

Round 68

1 On the World Wide Web, what country is represented by '.za'?

2 In Britain, which type of licence was introduced in 1946?

3 In the human body, where is the largest muscle?

4 According to the proverb, all roads lead to which Italian city?

5 In October 1959, Norwich became the first city in Britain to have what added to a postal address?

6 What nationality was Louis Braille, who invented the system of writing named after him?

7 In the animal kingdom, 'trapdoor' and 'nursery web' are both varieties of which creature?

8 In history, the highwayman Dick Turpin was hanged in which city?

9 What does 'PH' stand for on an Ordnance Survey map?

10 Which member of the pop band The Eurythmics directed the All Saints film *Honest*?

11 In the UK, if you dial an 0800 number, from a land line, how much are you charged per minute?

12 In which year was Alfred Hitchcock's film *Psycho* premiered in Los Angeles?

13 In the world of finance, what did PEP stand for?

14 In politics, Checkpoint Charlie was one of the main crossing points between the east and west of which divided European city?

15 Rhythmic versions of which sport involve the use of a hoop, ribbon, ball and rope?

16 Viti Levu is the largest of which group of islands?

17 In a standard game of Trivial Pursuit, which colour represents a geography question?

18 Which member of the royal family is chancellor of the University of Edinburgh?

19 'Mercury' and 'aneroid' are the two main types of which instrument that records pressure?

20 In the Bible, apart from Cain and Abel, who was Adam and Eve's other named son?

Previous Total

1,000

800

600

450

300

200

100

50

20

0

Banked

Total

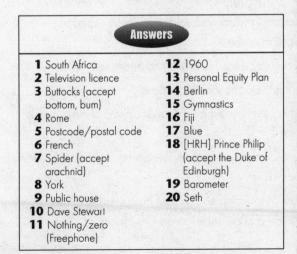

Answers

1 South Africa
2 Television licence
3 Buttocks (accept bottom, bum)
4 Rome
5 Postcode/postal code
6 French
7 Spider (accept arachnid)
8 York
9 Public house
10 Dave Stewart
11 Nothing/zero (Freephone)
12 1960
13 Personal Equity Plan
14 Berlin
15 Gymnastics
16 Fiji
17 Blue
18 [HRH] Prince Philip (accept the Duke of Edinburgh)
19 Barometer
20 Seth

1 In literature, which German author wrote the dramatic poem *Faust*?

2 The rose 'Elizabeth of Glamis' is named in honour of which member of the royal family?

3 In pre-decimal currency, how many half crowns made one pound?

4 In Europe, which country is the furthest north?

5 The rook and the jackdaw are members of which family of birds?

6 In science, which common unit is used to measure electric current?

7 In the 1927 film *The Jazz Singer*, who played the title role?

8 In language, which alphabet's first letter is 'aleph'?

9 In politics, in which year was the Greater London Council abolished?

10 In which city is the musical *42nd Street* set?

11 What is the opposite of 'concave'?

12 In which century did the Royal Academy of Arts open in London?

13 On which coast of the Mediterranean is the Italian resort of Rimini?

14 Which Shakespeare character has a mother called Gertrude and an uncle called Claudius?

15 In the painting the *Mona Lisa*, which usual facial feature is missing?

16 For what purpose is trinitrotoluene mainly used?

17 In the series of children's books, which character lives at 52 Festive Road?

18 How old was John F. Kennedy when he was sworn in as US president?

19 In film, whose first Hollywood screen test was assessed with the words 'Can't act. Slightly bald. Can dance a little'?

20 In the animal kingdom, 'ship' and 'Norway' are both types of which rodent?

Previous Total

1,000

800

600

450

300

200

100

50

20

0

Banked

Total

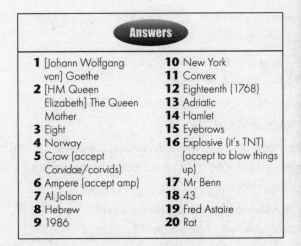

Answers

1 [Johann Wolfgang von] Goethe	**10** New York
2 [HM Queen Elizabeth] The Queen Mother	**11** Convex
	12 Eighteenth (1768)
	13 Adriatic
3 Eight	**14** Hamlet
4 Norway	**15** Eyebrows
5 Crow (accept Corvidae/corvids)	**16** Explosive (it's TNT) (accept to blow things up)
6 Ampere (accept amp)	**17** Mr Benn
7 Al Jolson	**18** 43
8 Hebrew	**19** Fred Astaire
9 1986	**20** Rat

Round 70

1 Which English higher-education institution is known by the initials UCL?

2 What form of mechanised transport was first introduced to New York in 1907?

3 In religion, the Prophet Muhammad, whose name means literally 'praised', was the first leader of which religion?

4 Who sang the theme tune of the 1973 Bond film *Live and Let Die*?

5 In the human body, how many anvils are there in each ear?

6 In which decade did Holyhead County Secondary School become Britain's first comprehensive school?

7 In literature, who wrote *Blott on the Landscape* and *Wilt*?

8 In history, in which year did the Soviet Union cease to exist?

9 In which US city might you visit the UN Headquarters and the Rockefeller Center?

10 Who sang 'The Power of Love' on the soundtrack of the 1985 film *Back to the Future*?

11 In maths, is the 'denominator' the number above or below the line in a fraction?

12 Which football striker, who finished as top scorer in the Premiership in 1999/2000, was named as the Carling Player of the Year?

13 In which building in Paris are Monet's water lily paintings, which he donated to the nation in the year of his death?

14 John Philip Sousa wrote the tune later used as the theme music for which television 'circus'?

15 Which astronaut was 77 years old when he went up in a space shuttle in 1998?

16 In the animal kingdom, what colour is a moorhen's beak?

17 The airport called 'Capodichino' serves which European city?

18 In which Shakespeare play would you find the character of Malvolio?

19 *Private Dancer* was an album released by which pop singer in 1984?

20 In which decade did Charles Strite first market his pop-up toaster?

Previous Total

1,000

800

600

450

300

200

100

50

20

0

Banked

Total

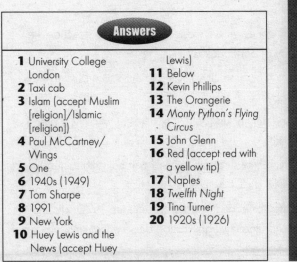

Answers

1 University College London
2 Taxi cab
3 Islam (accept Muslim [religion]/Islamic [religion])
4 Paul McCartney/ Wings
5 One
6 1940s (1949)
7 Tom Sharpe
8 1991
9 New York
10 Huey Lewis and the News (accept Huey Lewis)
11 Below
12 Kevin Phillips
13 The Orangerie
14 *Monty Python's Flying Circus*
15 John Glenn
16 Red (accept red with a yellow tip)
17 Naples
18 *Twelfth Night*
19 Tina Turner
20 1920s (1926)

1 Which dog has breeds called 'clumber' and 'cocker'?

2 Which actress starred in and sang the theme tune for the 1963 film *Move Over, Darling*?

3 The song 'Climb Every Mountain' features in which musical?

4 In the Olympic sport of beach volleyball, each medal match is the best of how many sets?

5 What is the usual French equivalent of the English word 'castle'?

6 Which crime novelist also writes under the name Barbara Vine?

7 Which 1959 Cliff Richard hit was written by Lionel Bart?

8 On the internet, what does the abbreviation FAQ stand for?

9 In science, what specific term is used to describe the study of earthquakes?

10 Which Scottish city is home to the statue of Greyfriars Bobby?

11 In the animal kingdom, the 'Chester white' is a breed of what?

12 Which English group for professional entertainers was formed on 1 July 1905?

13 In medicine, during which year in the 1970s did the World Health Organization declare that smallpox was eradicated?

14 In the television series, who played Sgt Dixon of Dock Green?

15 Which European city is known as 'the Venice of the North'?

16 Which female country-pop singer had a hit in 1999 with the song 'That Don't Impress Me Much'?

17 In Cambridgeshire, what is the local name for the River Cam?

18 In history, Stane Street was the name of the Roman road connecting London with which other city?

19 Which French painter is famous for his 1882 painting *A Bar at the Folies Bergère*?

20 What was the nationality of world champion gymnast Daniela Silivas?

Previous Total

( )

(1,000)

(800)

(600)

(450)

(300)

(200)

(100)

(50)

(20)

(0)

Banked

Total

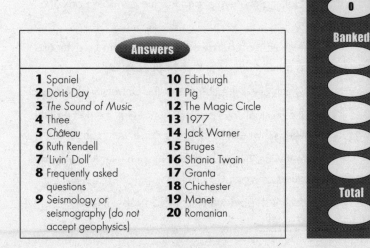

Answers

1 Spaniel	**10** Edinburgh
2 Doris Day	**11** Pig
3 *The Sound of Music*	**12** The Magic Circle
4 Three	**13** 1977
5 *Château*	**14** Jack Warner
6 Ruth Rendell	**15** Bruges
7 'Livin' Doll'	**16** Shania Twain
8 Frequently asked questions	**17** Granta
	18 Chichester
9 Seismology or seismography (*do not* accept geophysics)	**19** Manet
	20 Romanian

Round 72

1 Better known for his work with W. S. Gilbert, who composed the tune called 'St Gertrude' for the hymn 'Onward Christian Soldiers'?

2 In education, in which town is the University of Essex situated?

3 Which British leader wrote: 'It may almost be said, Before Alamein we never had a victory. After Alamein we never had a defeat'?

4 In literature, Graham Swift won the Booker Prize in 1996 for which novel?

5 In which county was the English composer Benjamin Britten born?

6 In food, which herb's name is derived from the Greek for 'king'?

7 In clothing, the eyelet and tongue are both parts of a what?

8 Which item of sportswear, typically worn by gymnasts, was named after a French trapeze artist?

9 In which city is the campus of the University of Warwick?

10 In the musical *My Fair Lady*, what was the name of the flower girl who was taught to cope with high society?

11 Greenwich Village and the Guggenheim Museum are features of which US city?

12 Which Irish poet won the 1995 Nobel Prize for Literature?

13 In the animal kingdom, from which continent does the yak come?

14 In history, of which country was Idi Amin head of state between 1971 and 1979?

15 Bodrum is a popular resort in which country?

16 In economics, for what do the letters IMF stand?

17 Was Britain's first space rocket called *Red Arrow* or *Blue Streak*?

18 In literature, complete the title of this Thomas Hardy novel: *Jude the . . .* what?

19 What is the capital of Scotland?

20 In the animal kingdom, which of these spiders is the most venomous, the 'false widow' or the 'black widow'?

Previous Total

1,000
800
600
450
300
200
100
50
20
0

Banked

Total

Answers

1 [Arthur] Sullivan (accept Sir Arthur Sullivan)
2 Colchester
3 [Sir] Winston Churchill
4 *Last Orders*
5 Suffolk
6 Basil
7 Shoe/boots
8 Leotard
9 Coventry
10 Eliza Doolittle (accept Liza Doolittle)
11 New York
12 Seamus Heaney (accept Heaney)
13 Asia
14 [Republic of] Uganda
15 Turkey
16 International Monetary Fund
17 *Blue Streak* (1964)
18 *Obscure*
19 Edinburgh
20 Black Widow

Round 73

1 Which *M* is a country on the southern coastline of Africa that suffered devastating floods in February and March 2000?

2 In flower arranging, what *O* is the trade name of a green block of light material used to hold cut flowers in place?

3 In the musical *West Side Story*, was Bernardo the leader of the Jets or the Sharks?

4 In the human body, is the aorta the largest artery or the largest vein?

5 Kathmandu is the capital of which country?

6 Does the island of Corfu lie in the Aegean or the Ionian Sea?

7 Complete the title of this 1980s Oscar-winning film by director Ingmar Bergman: *Fanny and . . .*?

8 What French term beginning with the letter *C* is given to a road closed at one end?

9 In the animal kingdom, is the head of the male mallard duck black or dark green?

10 What was the first name of Jenner, the inventor of the smallpox vaccination?

11 In history, the first Roman invasion of Britain took place in 55 BC under which military leader?

12 In the USA, Independence Hall is a feature of which Pennsylvanian city?

13 Complete the line of this nursery rhyme: 'Little Miss Muffet . . . '

14 Which poet wrote the poem *The Faerie Queene*, published in 1590, Spenser or Coleridge?

15 Who directed the film *Star Wars*?

16 In pop music, which band released the 1980s hit 'Karma Chameleon'?

17 In nature, do butterflies usually rest with their wings vertical or horizontal?

18 What S is the process of extracting metal from its ore by heating?

19 Which British military unit, known by a three-letter abbreviation, was founded by David Stirling, in 1941?

20 In which English county might you visit 'Earth Station Goonhilly'?

Previous Total

1,000

800

600

450

300

200

100

50

20

0

Banked

Total

Answers

1 Mozambique
2 Oasis
3 Sharks
4 Artery
5 Nepal
6 Ionian
7 *Alexander*
8 Cul-de-sac
9 Dark green
10 Edward
11 Julius Caesar (accept Gaius Julius Caesar; *do not* accept just Caesar)

12 Philadelphia
13 'Sat on a tuffet' (accept 'her tuffet')
14 Spenser
15 George Lucas
16 Culture Club
17 Vertical
18 Smelting
19 SAS (Special Air Service)
20 Cornwall

Round 74

1 In sport, which women's gymnastic exercise is always accompanied by music?

2 In ancient literature, was the playwright Aeschylus Greek or Roman?

3 In the UK, in which decade was the 30 miles per hour speed limit introduced nationally in built-up areas?

4 In nature, which *D* is the flower that's also called the Lent Lily?

5 In science, should a space rocket travel at 7 or 70 miles per second to leave Earth's atmosphere?

6 In which century was Great Ormond Street Hospital for Sick Children founded?

7 In architecture, 'herringbone bond' and 'stretcher bond' are types of what?

8 In geography, Latvia, Lithuania and which other republic make up the group known as the Baltic states?

9 Name one of the BBC television comedy series featuring the character Jim Hacker.

10 In the musical *The Sound of Music*, how many singing Von Trapp children were there?

11 In which English city might you visit the Albert Dock and the Pier Head?

12 Who composed the opera *Tosca*, first performed in the year 1900?

13 In food, what is the main ingredient of the dish bouillabaisse?

14 In history, in what year did the Bolsheviks seize power in Russia?

15 With whom did actress Nancy Davis co-star in the film *Hellcats of the Navy* and later marry?

16 The author Arthur C. Clarke was a radar instructor in which world war?

17 In the animal kingdom, a group of which felines is referred to as a 'leap'?

18 In the beauty industry, would a hairdresser or a manicurist use an emery board in their work?

19 In June 1999, Thabo Mbeki became president of which Commonwealth republic?

20 In astrology, the star sign Aquarius is represented by which image?

Previous Total

1,000

800

600

450

300

200

100

50

20

0

Banked

Total

Answers

1 Floor exercises (accept floor)
2 Greek
3 1930s (1935)
4 Daffodil
5 7 miles per second (escape velocity)
6 Nineteenth century (1852)
7 Brickwork/walls (accept masonry bonds)
8 Estonia
9 *Yes, Minister/Yes, Prime Minister*
10 Seven
11 Liverpool
12 [Giacomo] Puccini
13 Fish (accept shellfish)
14 1917
15 [President] Ronald Reagan
16 World War II
17 Leopards
18 Manicurist
19 [Republic of] South Africa
20 Water bearer/ carrier/pourer

1 Which Irish city is on the River Lagan?

2 In science, what *F* is the process of splitting an atom?

3 In language, which word describes both riding ocean waves and exploring the World Wide Web?

4 In ancient theatre, was Seneca a Greek or Roman playwright and philosopher?

5 In sport, the Penrith Lakes, Bondi Beach and Horsley Park were all venues for which major international event in 2000?

6 El Alamein, site of a battle that proved a turning point in World War II, is in which country?

7 In the human body, what *G* is a disease of the joints resulting from an accumulation of uric acid?

8 British designer John Galliano is head of which French fashion house?

9 Which author and illustrator wrote *The Snowman*?

10 In which decade did Kenneth Wood market the first food processor?

11 With which type of musical instrument is the name Steinway primarily associated?

12 'Long-eared' and 'pipistrelle' are both types of which animal?

13 Which further education examining body has its headquarters in Giltspur Street, London?

14 To which pop group did Louise Nurding belong before she went solo?

15 According to the proverb, what is the mother of invention?

16 In politics, on which occasion in 1990 did John Major declare, 'I am my own man'?

17 Which English Premiership club did former world footballer of the year George Weah join from Chelsea in July 2000?

18 In ancient history, from which country did the Zapotec people come: Mexico or Japan?

19 In which board game do the playing pieces include lead piping, rope and a spanner?

20 At sea level, is air pressure approximately fifteen or thirty pounds per square inch?

Previous Total

1,000

800

600

450

300

200

100

50

20

0

Banked

Total

Answers

1 Belfast
2 Fission
3 Surfing
4 Roman
5 Olympics
6 Egypt
7 Gout
8 Dior/Christian Dior
9 Raymond Briggs
10 1940s (1947)
11 Piano
12 Bat

13 City and Guilds
14 Eternal
15 Necessity
16 On succeeding Thatcher (accept on becoming prime minister)
17 Manchester City
18 Mexico
19 Cluedo
20 Fifteen

Round 76

1 In food, what French name is given to a sweet pancake served in a flaming sauce of orange liqueur?

2 In cricket, what score is known as a double Nelson?

3 In the animal kingdom, which male animal may be described as 'taurine' or 'bovine'?

4 In literature, the land of Lilliput features in which eighteenth-century novel?

5 In which century was the planet Pluto discovered?

6 In the television series *Steptoe & Son*, what was the name of the horse?

7 What is the world's smallest continent?

8 In nature, by what name is the crane-fly more commonly known?

9 In which classic 1946 film did an angel stop businessman George Bailey from committing suicide on Christmas Eve?

10 In classical music, what was Verdi's last opera called?

11 In politics, in which year did Ken Livingstone become leader of the Greater London Council?

12 Which stage musical features the character Norma Desmond?

13 In history, which Russian revolutionary leader arrived in St Petersburg, then called Petrograd, in a sealed train from Zurich in 1917?

14 Which colour clothing is particularly associated with royalty?

15 Which British national institution was founded in 1824 by Sir William Hillary?

16 Winston Smith is the central character in which novel?

17 Which pair of British comedians starred in the 1967 film *The Magnificent Two*?

18 In health, cholera is mainly spread in contaminated what?

19 Which Olympic 2000 sport had its headquarters at Rushcutters Bay, Sydney Harbour?

20 In the animal kingdom, 'teal' and 'gadwall' are both types of which bird?

Previous Total

( )
(1,000)
(800)
(600)
(450)
(300)
(200)
(100)
(50)
(20)
(0)

Banked
( )
( )
( )
( )
( )

Total
( )

Answers

1 Crêpe Suzette
2 222
3 Bull
4 *Gulliver's Travels*
5 Twentieth (1930)
6 Hercules
7 Australia
8 Daddy-long-legs
9 *It's a Wonderful Life*
10 *Falstaff*
11 1981
12 *Sunset Boulevard*
13 Lenin/Vladimir Ilich Ulyanov
14 Purple (accept crimson)
15 Royal National Lifeboat Institution (accept RNLI)
16 *1984*
17 Eric Morecambe and Ernie Wise
18 Water (*do not* accept food)
19 Sailing (accept yachting)
20 Duck (accept waterbird or waterfowl)

1 Which Spanish opera singer has recently become the Los Angeles Opera's artistic director?

2 In England, a PGCE is a postgraduate certificate in which subject?

3 In history, 'Operation Husky' was the codename for the Allied invasion of which Italian island in 1943?

4 In which present-day country was Nobel Prize-winner Mother Teresa born?

5 The film *Song of Norway* is based on the life of which composer?

6 The artist Vanessa Bell was the sister of which novelist?

7 In 1415, the battle of Agincourt took place between which two countries?

8 In which US city might you visit St Patrick's Cathedral and Wall Street?

9 Who directed the 1995 film *Braveheart*?

10 In which century was the telescope invented?

11 In sport, which nation was the surprise winner of the Euro 92 football championship?

12 From which musical does the song 'Consider Yourself' come?

13 In building, the sandstone 'Darley Dale', also known as Stancliffe, comes from which county?

14 In the human body, how many pairs of nasal bones are there?

15 Which actress is the mother of actor Larry Hagman?

16 The three sections of an insect's body are head, thorax and . . . what?

17 Darling Harbour and King's Cross are both districts of which Australian city?

18 Which Spanish writer, author of *The House of Bernardo Alba*, was shot by nationalists in 1936?

19 Sir Isaac Pitman's system of shorthand writing was first published in which century?

20 Which actor played the only juror to initially believe in the innocence of the defendant in the film *Twelve Angry Men*?

Previous Total

1,000
800
600
450
300
200
100
50
20
0

Banked

Total

Answers

1 Placido Domingo	**11** Denmark
2 Education/teaching	**12** *Oliver!*
3 Sicily	**13** Derbyshire
4 Macedonia	**14** One
5 Edvard Grieg	**15** Mary Martin
6 Virginia Woolf	**16** Abdomen
7 France and England (*do not* accept Britain)	**17** Sydney
8 New York	**18** Federico García Lorca
9 Mel Gibson	**19** Nineteenth century
10 Seventeenth century (1608)	**20** Henry Fonda

1 In fashion, which type of headwear is named after a Crimean battle?

2 Which dog has breeds called 'Brittany' and 'Welsh springer'?

3 Which movie star played Woody in the American television sitcom *Cheers*?

4 In science, how many atoms of hydrogen are there in one molecule of water?

5 In language, the French *'cochon'* is which animal in English?

6 Which investigative lawyer appeared in 89 novels by Erle Stanley Gardner?

7 Which horror actor performed the rap at the end of Michael Jackson's song 'Thriller'?

8 Holyroodhouse is a famous landmark in which city?

9 In English law, for what do the letters GBH stand?

10 In literature, who received the Booker Prize in 1981 for *Midnight's Children*?

11 What kind of fashion accessory was named after the actress Grace Kelly?

12 In the animal kingdom, the manta is a variety of which sea fish?

13 Murophobia is a fear of which animal?

14 In the television series *The Prisoner*, who starred as Number Six?

15 Which Norwegian town is known as the 'Gateway to the Fjords'?

16 Which composer wrote *Prelude to the Afternoon of a Faun* in 1894?

17 In literature, which famous, female Greek love poet lived on the island of Lesbos?

18 In art, which Italian term for 'pity' is applied to a painting or sculpture of the Virgin Mary with the dead Christ on her lap?

19 Name one of the male actors who dressed up as women musicians in the 1959 film *Some Like it Hot*.

20 Which city's former polytechnic has become the University of Northumbria?

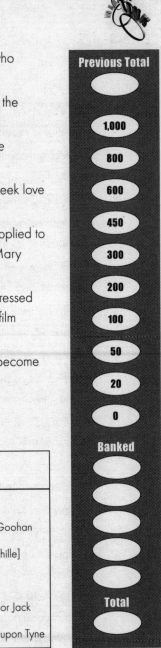

Previous Total

1,000

800

600

450

300

200

100

50

20

0

Banked

Total

Answers

1 Balaclava [helmet]	**12** Ray
2 Spaniel	**13** Mice
3 Woody Harrelson	**14** Patrick McGoohan
4 Two	**15** Bergen
5 Pig	**16** [Claude Achille] Debussy
6 Perry Mason	**17** Sappho
7 Vincent Price	**18** *Pietà*
8 Edinburgh	**19** Tony Curtis or Jack Lemmon
9 Grievous bodily harm	
10 [Salman] Rushdie	**20** Newcastle upon Tyne
11 Handbag/Kelly bag	

Round 79

1 In World War II, what was the nickname of Air Marshal Sir Arthur Harris?

2 What nationality is the famous fashion designer Kenzo?

3 Which actor played the jewel thief Sir Charles Litton in the 1963 film *The Pink Panther*?

4 In fashion, where on the body would you wear a pillbox?

5 Which television writer's works included *Pennies From Heaven* and *The Singing Detective*?

6 Which American document consists of seven Articles, the Bill of Rights and the Amendments?

7 In music, what was pop star Little Richard's surname?

8 Which future president of France was the leader of the Free French forces during World War II?

9 In the UK, what are the first two letters in Leeds postcodes?

10 In World War II, 'Operation Barbarossa' was the codename for the German invasion of which country?

11 In politics, Kate Hoey replaced Tony Banks in July 1999 as minister for what?

12 Who wrote the 1994 autobiography *A Long Walk to Freedom*?

13 In film, whose Oscar acceptance speech, for the 1993 film *Philadelphia*, included the words 'the streets of heaven are too crowded with angels'?

14 In UK education, Napier University is situated in which British city?

15 In fashion, which item has a tongue and an instep?

16 In which sport did Paul Palmer represent Great Britain at the Sydney 2000 Olympics: swimming or running?

17 Which word can mean 'a charlatan' or 'the cry of a duck'?

18 Hialeah and Coral Gables are suburbs of which Florida city?

19 In which Portugese region is the city of Faro a major destination?

20 In the animal kingdom, does a hedgehog lay eggs?

Previous Total

1,000
800
600
450
300
200
100
50
20
0

Banked

Total

Answers

1 'Bomber' [Harris]	**11** Sport
2 Japanese	**12** [Nelson] Mandela
3 David Niven	**13** Tom Hanks
4 Head	**14** Edinburgh
5 Dennis Potter	**15** Shoe/boot/slipper
6 The Constitution	**16** Swimming
7 Penniman	**17** Quack
8 [Charles] de Gaulle	**18** Miami
9 LS	**19** Algarve
10 Soviet Union (accept Russia/USSR)	**20** No

Round 80

1 Poldark Mine is a tourist attraction in which English county?

2 Was the religious movement Confucianism founded before or after Christianity?

3 Which actor dressed up as the character Dorothy Michaels in the 1982 film *Tootsie*?

4 In physics, which is lighter, a proton or an electron?

5 The holder of which political office is also, technically, the Commander-in-Chief of the American armed forces?

6 What is the name of the character played by Patricia Routledge in the television series *Keeping Up Appearances*?

7 In literature, complete the title of this 1945 novel by French author Jean-Paul Sartre: *The Age of . . .* what?

8 Did Halley's Comet last appear in 1986 or 1996?

9 Complete the next line of this nursery rhyme: 'Jack and Jill went up the hill . . .'

10 Is the chemical element silicon represented by the symbol Si or Sl?

11 What *L* are the leather shorts traditionally worn in Austria?

12 In pop music, what is the first name of Scary Spice?

13 Which actress played the part of Sandy in the 1978 film *Grease*?

14 In the House of Commons, who became Father of the House in 1992?

15 In sport, what nationality are the tennis players Venus and Serena Williams?

16 Was classical composer Ralph Vaughan Williams born in England or Wales?

17 In transport, what type of vehicle is a frigate?

18 In literature, in which country is James Clavell's novel *Shogun* set?

19 In maths, what is 25 per cent of 200?

20 Which of the Queen's country residences lies on the River Dee?

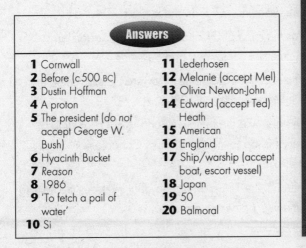

Previous Total

1,000

800

600

450

300

200

100

50

20

0

Banked

Total

Answers

1 Cornwall
2 Before (c.500 BC)
3 Dustin Hoffman
4 A proton
5 The president (*do not* accept George W. Bush)
6 Hyacinth Bucket
7 *Reason*
8 1986
9 'To fetch a pail of water'
10 Si
11 Lederhosen
12 Melanie (accept Mel)
13 Olivia Newton-John
14 Edward (accept Ted) Heath
15 American
16 England
17 Ship/warship (accept boat, escort vessel)
18 Japan
19 50
20 Balmoral

Round 81

1 Was Bill Clinton the 42nd, the 44th, or the 46th president of the United States?

2 In nature, are 'woodland grayling' and 'meadow brown' species of orchid or butterfly?

3 In which century did the English poet Percy Shelley die?

4 What *A* is a bridge which carries water?

5 Which actress played the part of Annie in the 1994 film *Speed*?

6 The Maori people are the original inhabitants of which country?

7 In food, the zest refers to what part of a citrus fruit?

8 In music, what nationality is folk singer Joan Baez?

9 What *L* is the Scottish equivalent of the English word 'lord'?

10 In medicine, for what do the letters HRT stand?

11 Was the musical *Oklahoma* written by Rogers and Hammerstein or Gilbert and Sullivan?

12 Who succeeded Geoffrey Howe as foreign secretary after his resignation in 1989?

13 In history, was the famous World War I pilot William Avery Bishop (a.k.a. Bill Bishop) Canadian or American?

14 In the UK the TTA is an agency that oversees the training of members of which profession?

15 What term is used to describe independent, fee-paying schools which educate children up to university entrance standard?

16 In the animal kingdom, 'bean' and 'greylag' are both types of which bird?

17 Berne is the capital of which country?

18 Is the chemical element chlorine represented by the symbol Ch, Cl or Cr?

19 In football, which Spanish team did Gary Lineker join in 1986?

20 On books, what is the International Standard Book Number better known as?

Previous Total

1,000

800

600

450

300

200

100

50

20

0

Banked

Total

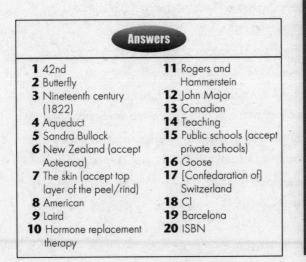

Answers

1 42nd
2 Butterfly
3 Nineteenth century (1822)
4 Aqueduct
5 Sandra Bullock
6 New Zealand (accept Aotearoa)
7 The skin (accept top layer of the peel/rind)
8 American
9 Laird
10 Hormone replacement therapy

11 Rogers and Hammerstein
12 John Major
13 Canadian
14 Teaching
15 Public schools (accept private schools)
16 Goose
17 [Confedaration of] Switzerland
18 Cl
19 Barcelona
20 ISBN

Round 82

1 In the human body, is the lingual artery in the hand or in the neck?

2 If the first note of the music scale is doh, what is the fifth note of the scale?

3 Which London church stands at the top of Ludgate Hill?

4 In food, the tamarillo fruit is also known as the 'tree . . .' what?

5 The Ayatollah Khomeini was leader of which country between 1979 and 1989?

6 In music, which group wrote the songs 'Whole Lotta Love' and 'Stairway to Heaven'?

7 What is the first name of Michael Caine's wife?

8 What is the motto of the SAS?

9 According to the literal meaning, a bibliophile is a person who has a love of what?

10 In the animal kingdom, *Cygnus* is the Latin name for which bird?

11 What A is Africa's second-largest country, stretching from the Mediterranean coast deep into the Sahara desert?

12 In British history, which laws, which had previously controlled movements of grain, were repealed in 1846?

13 In astrology, the crab is the symbol for which sign of the zodiac?

14 In sport, how many Olympic gold medals did Jesse Owens win in 1936?

15 Mycology is the study of what: fungi or the sinus?

16 Halkidiki is a popular tourist destination in which country?

17 Between the two world wars, which country built the Maginot Line, intended as a defence against German attack?

18 Which actor played Axel Foley in the 1984 film *Beverly Hills Cop*?

19 In the human body, the adrenal glands lie at the upper end of which organ?

20 Which American television soap featured the characters Miss Ellie and Clayton Farlow?

Previous Total

1,000

800

600

450

300

200

100

50

20

0

Banked

Total

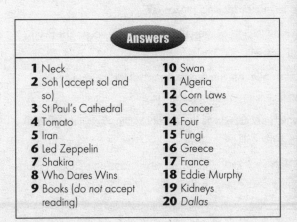

Answers

1 Neck
2 Soh (accept sol and so)
3 St Paul's Cathedral
4 Tomato
5 Iran
6 Led Zeppelin
7 Shakira
8 Who Dares Wins
9 Books (*do not* accept reading)
10 Swan
11 Algeria
12 Corn Laws
13 Cancer
14 Four
15 Fungi
16 Greece
17 France
18 Eddie Murphy
19 Kidneys
20 *Dallas*

Round 83

1 Which vitamin is also known by the name of 'tocopherol'?

2 What are the first names of the parents of fashion designer Jasper Conran?

3 Which American ex-president's wife published a collection of love letters from her devoted husband in September 2000?

4 In literature, James Bigglesworth, known as Biggles, was a daredevil aviator created by which author?

5 In what century was the drug aspirin first developed?

6 Which R describes an animal that chews the cud?

7 In which capital city might you visit Union Station and the US Capitol Building?

8 What is the name of the present Russian president?

9 Which P is an alloy of tin and lead which was often used to make drinking tankards?

10 From which part of the UK does the opera singer Bryn Terfel come?

11 Is British Summer Time one hour behind or one hour ahead of Greenwich Mean Time?

12 In which decade was the comedy film The Life of Brian released?

13 In which year did UK Labour politician James Callaghan become prime minister?

14 In the US, what was closed on Alcatraz island in 1963?

15 Which is the only continent with no permanent human population?

16 What beats Scissors in the Paper, Scissors, Stone game?

17 Which name for the Devil means 'lord of the flies'?

18 What is the first name of the Scottish missionary Livingstone, who explored East and Central Africa?

19 When Richard Nixon resigned in 1974, who replaced him as US president?

20 What is the name of the old-fashioned bicycle with a very large front wheel and a very small back wheel?

Previous Total

◯

1,000

800

600

450

300

200

100

50

20

0

Banked

◯

◯

◯

◯

◯

Total

◯

Answers

1 Vitamin E	**12** 1970s (1979)
2 Terence and Shirley	**13** 1976
3 Nancy Reagan	**14** Prison/jail
4 [Captain W. E.] Johns	**15** Antarctica
5 Nineteenth	**16** Stone
6 Ruminant	**17** Beelzebub (accept
7 Washington, DC	Beelzebul)
8 [Vladimir] Putin	**18** David
9 Pewter	**19** [Gerald Rudolph]
10 Wales	Ford
11 One hour ahead	**20** Penny farthing

Round 84

1 What is the name of the BBC documentary about people living on an island off the coast of Scotland?

2 In history, the 'Anzac' was a combined army corps formed between which two countries during World War I?

3 In the animal kingdom, an 'English Romney' is a type of what?

4 In sport, what colour is the background to the Olympic flag?

5 In Italy, which Venetian bridge links the Doge's Palace to the state prison?

6 Which classical composer wrote the nineteenth-century opera *Otello*, first performed in 1887?

7 In literature, who is the author son of Kingsley Amis?

8 What is the first name of the wife of television interviewer Michael Parkinson?

9 In business, what does AGM stand for?

10 Which actor played Dr Bamford in the British film *Saving Grace*?

11 Jomo Kenyatta was the first president of which country?

12 In ancient Egypt, the pyramids were built as tombs for whom?

13 Which country's ruler was forced to renounce his divinity after the Second World War, although he kept the title of emperor?

14 In literature, what was the surname of the poets Dante, Gabriel and Christina?

15 Which actress played Velvet Brown in the 1944 film *National Velvet*?

16 On the World Wide Web, which country is represented by '.pl'?

17 Which 1980s pop band recorded the album *Welcome to the Pleasure Dome*?

18 Cynophobia is a fear of which animals?

19 In the children's television programme, what type of building did Portland Bill live in?

20 Maputo is the capital city of which African country?

Previous Total

( )

1,000

800

600

450

300

200

100

50

20

0

Banked

( )
( )
( )
( )
( )

Total

( )

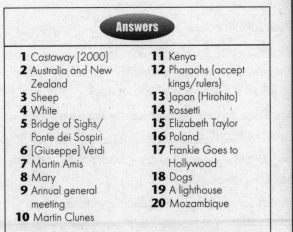

Answers

1 Castaway [2000]
2 Australia and New Zealand
3 Sheep
4 White
5 Bridge of Sighs/ Ponte dei Sospiri
6 [Giuseppe] Verdi
7 Martin Amis
8 Mary
9 Annual general meeting
10 Martin Clunes

11 Kenya
12 Pharaohs (accept kings/rulers)
13 Japan (Hirohito)
14 Rossetti
15 Elizabeth Taylor
16 Poland
17 Frankie Goes to Hollywood
18 Dogs
19 A lighthouse
20 Mozambique

Round 85

1 In which European country did women finally win the right to vote in national elections after a referendum held in February 1971?

2 In which film did Jack Nicholson play the Devil, who seduces three women?

3 In first aid, a 'triangular' and 'roller' are both types of what?

4 What is the capital of Malta?

5 In modern literature, who wrote the 1984 novel *The Fourth Protocol*?

6 In UK history, which king said at his trial, 'I do stand more for the liberty of my people, than any here'?

7 What is the largest borough in New York City?

8 Which television cop did Telly Savallas play in the 1970s?

9 Which French sculptor's works include *The Burghers of Calais*?

10 In medicine, the general anaesthetic Halothane was discovered in England in which decade?

11 Jimmy Page and Robert Plant were members of which British rock band?

12 In the animal kingdom, the 'monk' and 'ribbon' are both types of which mammal?

13 In which country did Zen Buddhism originate?

14 What is the official language of Kenya?

15 Neil Pearson played Detective Tony Clark in which television series?

16 Adam Clayton and Larry Mullen Junior are members of which Irish pop group?

17 What was the nickname of King Louis XIV of France?

18 The song 'All That Jazz' comes from which musical?

19 From which country did Erik Rotheim, the inventor of the aerosol, come?

20 If you were born on 1 October, what star sign would you be?

Previous Total

1,000

800

600

450

300

200

100

50

20

0

Banked

Total

Answers

1 [Confederation of] Switzerland
2 *The Witches of Eastwick*
3 Bandages
4 Valletta
5 Frederick Forsyth
6 Charles I
7 Queens
8 [Lt Theo] Kojak
9 [Auguste] Rodin
10 1950s (1951)

11 Led Zeppelin
12 Seal
13 China
14 Swahili
15 *Between the Lines*
16 U2
17 The Sun King (accept *Le Roi Soleil*)
18 *Chicago*
19 Norway
20 Libra

Round 86

1 What was the name of the German air force during World War II?

2 Name one of the female stars from the BBC television sitcom *Men Behaving Badly*.

3 The main square in Venice is named after which saint?

4 Which 1994 Michael Crichton novel, about sexual harrassment, was turned into a film starring Demi Moore?

5 What is the usual English name for the animal the French call a *'cheval'*?

6 In space, the name of what type of stellar phenomenon means 'new' in Latin?

7 The male of which large animal may be called a 'boomer' or an 'old man': a kangaroo or a gorilla?

8 In transport, for what does HGV stand?

9 The characters of Tallulah and Fat Sam featured in which 1970s film musical?

10 Which artist and poet wrote the lines 'Tyger! Tyger! burning bright in the forests of the night'?

11 Which actor played George III in the 1994 film *The Madness of King George*?

12 In history, which country had Tunisia as a colony from the 1880s until 1956?

13 In literature, which former Poet Laureate wrote a collection of poems called *Birthday Letters* about his marriage to Sylvia Plath?

14 From which central Asian country would a car with an 'AFG' sticker come?

15 Which European city is home to the oldest university in the western world?

16 In the novel *Goodbye Mr Chips*, what is the hero's profession?

17 In television, what was the name of the dog in *The Magic Roundabout*?

18 Which children's author wrote the *Malory Towers* series?

19 The 'Alaskan malamute' is a breed of which type of animal?

20 In classical music, who composed the opera *William Tell* in 1829?

Previous Total

1,000
800
600
450
300
200
100
50
20
0

Banked

Total

Answers

1 Luftwaffe
2 Leslie Ash or Caroline Quentin
3 Saint Mark (accept San Marco)
4 *Disclosure*
5 Horse
6 Nova
7 Kangaroo
8 Heavy goods vehicle
9 *Bugsy Malone*
10 William Blake
11 Nigel Hawthorne
12 France
13 Ted Hughes (accept Edward James Hughes)
14 Afghanistan
15 Bologna
16 Schoolteacher/ teaching/ schoolmaster
17 Dougal
18 Enid Blyton
19 Dog (husky)
20 Rossini

Round 87

1 In the beauty industry, which M is a professional carer for hands and fingernails?

2 In music, is a piccolo a woodwind or a string instrument?

3 In which decade was the actress Dame Judi Dench born?

4 Would you find the alimentary canal on the moon or in the human body?

5 In which decade was instant coffee invented?

6 In science, is 'plumbago' another name for graphite or for camphor?

7 Paella is a traditional dish of which country?

8 What is the largest of the Balearic islands?

9 Which musical, set in Vietnam, is based on the story of *Madama Butterfly*?

10 In modern science, is time the first, second, third or fourth dimension?

11 In clothing, would a cowboy wear his chaps above or below the waist?

12 Which actor played Danny in the 1978 film *Grease*?

13 With which of Her Majesty's Forces does Prince Andrew serve?

14 In science, did Ernest Rutherford propose the nuclear model of the atom in the year 1911 or 1921?

15 In history, which Scottish king won the Battle of Bannockburn in the year 1314?

16 What is the main religion of Morocco?

17 In music, which is the lower female voice, soprano or contralto?

18 In America, PA is the postal abbreviation for which state?

19 In the UK, what type of transport is a Green Goddess?

20 In nutrition, both wheatgerm and broccoli are rich sources of folic . . . what?

Previous Total

1,000

800

600

450

300

200

100

50

20

0

Banked

Total

Answers

1 Manicurist
2 Woodwind
3 1930s (1934)
4 Human body
5 1930s
6 Graphite (carbon)
7 Spain
8 Majorca (Mallorca)
9 *Miss Saigon*
10 Fourth
11 Below (chaps are leather protection for the front of the legs)

12 John Travolta
13 Royal Navy
14 1911
15 Robert the Bruce (accept Robert I of Scotland)
16 Islam/Muslim
17 Contralto
18 Pennsylvania
19 Fire engine (accept army fire engine)
20 Acid

1 Complete the title of the 1980s children's television programme: *Ragdolly . . .* who?

2 Which character was played by Clint Eastwood in the television series *Rawhide*?

3 Complete the first line of this nursery rhyme: 'Hey diddle diddle, . . .'

4 In history, what *A* was the central area of an ancient Roman amphitheatre used for gladiators to fight?

5 In the 1988 comedy film *A Fish Called Wanda*, which actress played Wanda?

6 In which African country are the cities Pretoria and Bloemfontein?

7 In art, what *P* is the name given to paintings which show a visual likeness of someone's face?

8 In nature, what is the name given to the waxy, water-repellent coating of a leaf?

9 In politics, in 1990, who replaced Nigel Lawson as Chancellor of the Exchequer?

10 In science, does the chemical element mercury expand or contract when it is heated?

11 In history, how many times did Stanley Baldwin serve as prime minister of Britain?

12 In maths, does a scalene triangle have three equal or unequal sides?

13 Who won the Eurovision Song Contest for Britain in 1976 with 'Save Your Kisses For Me'?

14 How is the footballer Luiz de Nazario di Lima better known?

15 What nationality is Douglas Coupland, author of the 1991 novel *Generation X*?

16 In 1961, did President Kennedy announce the start of the *Apollo* or the *Challenger* space programme?

17 Which large cat is known as 'the king of beasts'?

18 The haj is a pilgrimage made by a Muslim to which city?

19 Which 1996 musical film, set in Argentina, starred Antonio Banderas?

20 In the animal kingdom, the adult of which species of bird is larger: a goose or a swan?

Previous Total

1,000

800

600

450

300

200

100

50

20

0

Banked

Total

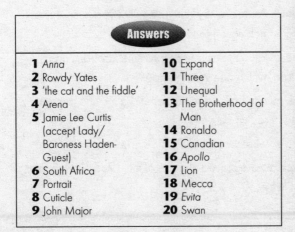

Answers

1 *Anna*
2 Rowdy Yates
3 'the cat and the fiddle'
4 Arena
5 Jamie Lee Curtis (accept Lady/ Baroness Haden-Guest)
6 South Africa
7 Portrait
8 Cuticle
9 John Major
10 Expand
11 Three
12 Unequal
13 The Brotherhood of Man
14 Ronaldo
15 Canadian
16 *Apollo*
17 Lion
18 Mecca
19 *Evita*
20 Swan

1 Who co-starred with Walter Matthau in the 1968 film *The Odd Couple*?

2 Which city is home to John Knox's House and the Royal Mile?

3 In food, from which country do tapas bars originate?

4 Which actor has twice been married to Melanie Griffith and twice split up with her?

5 *Notes From a Small Island* is a book by Bill Bryson about which country?

6 In the animal kingdom, are the legs of a partridge bare or feathery?

7 In which European country was the writer Hans Christian Andersen born?

8 In UK politics, who was the Labour Party's longest-serving prime minister?

9 In which Asian country during the 1930s did the famous 'Long March' take place?

10 In the children's television programme *Roobarb and Custard*, which one was the dog?

11 In the human body, does diphtheria affect the respiratory or the digestive system?

12 In travel, what was the De Havilland Comet?

13 Which actress played The Girl in the 1955 film *The Seven Year Itch*?

14 Which group of islands is the furthest north of all Britain's islands?

15 Which comic actress was married to Tom Arnold and starred in a sitcom named after her?

16 In language, does the French phrase *'à la carte'* translate as 'from the menu' or 'from the table'?

17 Which imperial weight measurement is also another name for the snow-leopard?

18 Name the Australian who is the main presenter of BBC television's *Animal Hospital*.

19 Complete the title of this Arthur Miller play, *Death of a . . .* what?

20 Which London Academy was founded in 1822 whose past students include Sir Henry Wood and Sir Simon Rattle?

Previous Total

1,000

800

600

450

300

200

100

50

20

0

Banked

Total

Answers

1 Jack Lemmon	**13** Marilyn Monroe
2 Edinburgh	**14** Shetland Islands
3 Spain	**15** Roseanne Arnold
4 Don Johnson	(accept Roseanne)
5 UK/Britain	**16** 'From the menu'
6 Bare	**17** The ounce
7 Denmark	**18** Rolf Harris
8 Harold Wilson	**19** *Salesman*
9 China	**20** Royal Academy of
10 Roobarb	Music
11 Respiratory	
12 Aeroplane (accept	
commercial passenger	
jet)	

Round 90

1 Which Ken Kesey novel, set in a mental hospital, became an Oscar-winning film?

2 Which organisation was founded by Robert Baden Powell in 1908?

3 In which modern-day country was Queen Victoria's husband, Prince Albert, born in 1819?

4 In astronomy, is Earth the second or third planet from the sun in the solar system?

5 Does England or the Republic of Ireland have the larger population?

6 In the workplace, what do the initials AOB stand for on agendas and minutes?

7 In film, who sang the 1981 Bond theme tune 'For Your Eyes Only'?

8 In which region of Italy have Tony Blair and his family spent their last two summer holidays?

9 What is the official language of Mozambique?

10 What S is the word commonly used in Australia for a person in charge of cattle or other livestock?

11 Which comedian was born in England, Stan Laurel or Oliver Hardy?

12 In religion, in which country did Sikhism originate?

13 Thomas Jones Woodward is the birth name of which Welsh pop icon?

14 From which country would a car with an 'E' sticker come?

15 What is the more common name for the Chinese gooseberry?

16 On average, do lions live longer in the wild or in captivity?

17 In astrology, the star sign Sagittarius is represented by which image?

18 In literature, 'How the Leopard Got Its Spots' is part of which Kipling story collection?

19 The song by Survivor 'Eye of the Tiger' was the theme to the third in which series of films?

20 In UK television, what are the surnames of the comedy duo Vic and Bob?

Previous Total

1,000

800

600

450

300

200

100

50

20

0

Banked

Total

Round 91

1 Before reunification, the German Democratic Republic was commonly known as what?

2 Brendan Foster is now a leading television commentator on which sporting activity?

3 To a reproduction of which painting did artist Marcel Duchamp famously add a moustache and a beard?

4 Which seventeenth-century English poet wrote a poem about his blindness?

5 In politics, the Suez Crisis followed which country's nationalisation of the Suez Canal?

6 Which actor played Count Lazlo Almasy in the 1996 film *The English Patient*?

7 On the World Wide Web, which country is represented by '.ch'?

8 In food, 'silverside' is a British cut of which meat?

9 In the children's television show, which Teletubby loves to wear his hat?

10 In geography, the Yellow Sea is an inlet of which ocean?

11 In history, the politician George Lansbury was a member of which party?

12 In UK politics, who first challenged Margaret Thatcher for the leadership of the Conservative Party in 1990?

13 In which film did the Beatles first appear together?

14 In classical music, in which European city did the composer Chopin die?

15 Which artist's daughter Paloma is a jewellery designer and scent creator?

16 Diwali is a major festival in which religion?

17 In history, Khalid served as king of which country from 1975 until his death?

18 In film, which English actress played Miss Kenton in the 1993 period drama *The Remains of the Day*?

19 How many adrenal glands are there in the human body?

20 Which 'tea-clipper' is on display at Greenwich?

Previous Total

1,000

800

600

450

300

200

100

50

20

0

Banked

Total

Answers

1 East Germany	**12** Michael Heseltine
2 Athletics	**13** *A Hard Day's Night*
3 *Mona Lisa*	**14** Paris
4 John Milton	**15** Pablo Picasso
5 Egypt's	**16** Hinduism or Sikhism
6 Ralph Fiennes	(accept Jainism)
7 Switzerland	**17** Saudi Arabia
8 Beef	**18** Emma Thompson
9 Dipsy	**19** Two
10 Pacific	**20** *Cutty Sark*
11 British Labour Party	

Round 92

1 On a UK road sign, what does a red car and a black car inside a red circle mean?

2 In food, when milk is made into cheese, it is separated into two parts. Name one.

3 In the animal kingdom, the 'black Norfolk' is a breed of what?

4 Which actor co-starred with George Cole in the television series *Minder*?

5 In the television soap opera *Dallas*, which character was played by Larry Hagman?

6 In classical music, who composed the opera *Aida*?

7 In ancient history, Latium was an area in the central part of which European country?

8 Who sang 'Good Morning' with Gene Kelly and Donald O'Connor in *Singin' in the Rain*?

9 What was the first name of the English explorer Captain Scott who died in the Antarctic?

10 In film, in which country was the 1987 period drama *White Mischief* set?

11 In which decade was the Breathalyser introduced in Britain?

12 The election for the President of the United States of America is held once every how many years?

13 Former *Baywatch* star Pamela Anderson was married to which American rocker?

14 Which architect was responsible for the Brighton Pavilion, Marble Arch and the remodelled Buckingham Palace?

15 In the animal kingdom, the gibbon is native to which continent?

16 In television's *EastEnders*, what is the name of the family who moved into 23 Albert Square in September 2000?

17 Which American museum, opened in 1974 in Malibu, California, is a replica of a Roman villa?

18 In boxing, who defeated Sonny Liston in 1964 to become World Heavyweight Champion for the first time?

19 In which children's television programme were the characters Dobbin, Mr Claypole and Hazel the McWitch?

20 Which modern classic novel by Evelyn Waugh is narrated by Charles Ryder and features Sebastian Flyte?

Previous Total

1,000

800

600

450

300

200

100

50

20

0

Banked

Total

Answers

1 No overtaking	**12** Four
2 Curds or whey	**13** Tommy Lee
3 Turkey	**14** John Nash
4 Dennis Waterman	**15** Asia
5 J. R. Ewing (accept J. R.)	**16** The Slaters
6 [Giuseppe] Verdi	**17** Getty Museum
7 Italy	**18** Muhammad Ali (accept Cassius Clay)
8 Debbie Reynolds	**19** *Rent-a-ghost*
9 Robert	**20** *Brideshead Revisited*
10 Kenya	
11 1960s	

Round 93

1 Which desert covers much of north-west Africa?

2 In the year 2000, which American singer asked the UN to shut down a pornographic website which shared her name?

3 In which year was the television series *Only Fools and Horses* first broadcast?

4 In geography, Freetown is the capital of which African country?

5 Which former Beatle wrote the song 'Working Class Hero'?

6 In an American restaurant, which term describes a dish containing both seafood and meat?

7 Which state in America is the biggest oil producer?

8 Who is the author of the anthropological book *The Naked Ape*?

9 In which Canadian city is McGill University?

10 Novelist James Joyce was born in Ireland and died in which country?

11 What colour is the cross on the Swiss flag?

12 Playwright Alan Ayckbourn is the artistic director of the Stephen Joseph Theatre in which town?

13 In medicine, which organ is affected by Bright's disease?

14 In fashion, what is the British name for the hat known to Americans as a 'derby'?

15 What is the name of the square-mile district in London, between Oxford Street and Shaftesbury Avenue, famous for its nightlife?

16 What nationality was the author Franz Kafka?

17 In building, from which county does Delabole slate come?

18 In which English town is the main site of Brunel University?

19 In which year did the aviator Louis Blériot first fly over the English Channel?

20 Which actress played Suzie in the 1989 film *The Fabulous Baker Boys*?

Previous Total

1,000

800

600

450

300

200

100

50

20

0

Banked

Total

Answers

1 Sahara	**13** Kidney
2 Madonna	**14** Bowler
3 1981	**15** Soho
4 Sierra Leone	**16** Czech (accept
5 John Lennon	Bohemian: he was
6 Surf 'n' turf	born in Prague, which
7 Alaska	was then part of
8 Desmond Morris	Bohemia)
9 Montreal	**17** Cornwall
10 Switzerland	**18** Uxbridge (do not
11 White (red	accept Middlesex)
background)	**19** 1909
12 Scarborough	**20** Michelle Pfeiffer

Round 94

1 In maths, add $4\frac{1}{2}$ to $5\frac{1}{2}$.

2 In nature, does the duck-billed platypus give birth to live young, or lay eggs?

3 What *A* is the name given to the female superior of a nunnery or convent?

4 The San Andreas fault runs for over 600 miles across which American state?

5 Which British singer's albums have included *Faith* and *Listen Without Prejudice*?

6 In ancient literature, was Horace a Roman or a Greek poet?

7 In 1970, who succeeded Nasser as president of Egypt?

8 What *P* is the term applied to insecticides, fungicides and herbicides?

9 In which 1980s time-travelling trilogy of films did Michael J. Fox star?

10 In the animal kingdom, is a drake a male or female duck?

11 Of which Asian country is Kabul the capital?

12 'Good Morning Starshine' and 'Aquarius' are songs from which 1960s musical?

13 In clothing, what *L* is the folded-back continuation of a jacket collar?

14 How many moons does the planet Mars have, one or two?

15 In politics, what *R* means to formally approve or confirm something?

16 In snooker, what is the maximum break achievable without penalties: 147 or 160?

17 In which Handel oratorio does the Hallelujah Chorus appear?

18 On which Mediterranean island would you find the towns of Larnaca, Limassol and Nicosia?

19 In literature, according to a Dickens novel first published in 1859, it was a tale of how many cities?

20 Add 14 to the square root of 49.

Previous Total

1,000

800

600

450

300

200

100

50

20

0

Banked

Total

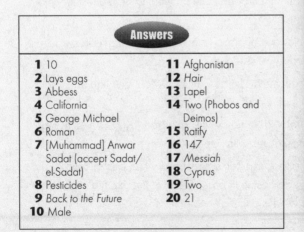

Answers

1 10
2 Lays eggs
3 Abbess
4 California
5 George Michael
6 Roman
7 [Muhammad] Anwar Sadat (accept Sadat/ el-Sadat)
8 Pesticides
9 *Back to the Future*
10 Male
11 Afghanistan
12 *Hair*
13 Lapel
14 Two (Phobos and Deimos)
15 Ratify
16 147
17 *Messiah*
18 Cyprus
19 Two
20 21

Round 95

1 In 1960, Nan Winton was the first woman on BBC television to do what?

2 Does the USA contain approximately 5, 15, or 20 per cent of the world's population?

3 In science, what C is used to speed up chemical reactions, without itself changing?

4 In the title of a Shakespeare play, what creature is being tamed?

5 Who is the designer who established the Habitat stores in 1964?

6 In film, Kathy Bates starred as The Unsinkable Molly Brown in which James Cameron movie?

7 In which country was the model Claudia Schiffer born?

8 What is the name of ground almond paste used in cake decoration?

9 Inside the European Union, what is the highest mountain range?

10 Which flower has a Latin name meaning 'little sword', because of its leaves?

11 Which metal is most commonly found in liquid thermometers?

12 What V is the hardening of rubber by heating it at high temperatures with sulphur?

13 In sailing, what's the term used when a boat follows a zig-zag course in order to sail in the direction from which the wind is coming?

14 Name the Australian outlaw of the 1870s who became famous for the home-made armour he wore during his robberies?

15 Which English city would you find between the rivers Plym and Tamar?

16 In literature, who wrote verses and stories for his son, Christopher Robin?

17 In the animal kingdom, is a vixen a fox or a rabbit?

18 Alex Salmond resigned as leader of which UK political party in July 2000?

19 In which event did Jason Queally become Britain's first gold medallist of the Sydney 2000 Olympics: shooting or cycling?

20 Name the author of the 1932 classic novel *Brave New World*.

Previous Total

1,000
800
600
450
300
200
100
50
20
0

Banked

Total

Answers

1 Read the news (in vision)
2 5 per cent
3 Catalyst
4 Shrew
5 Sir Terence Conran (accept Conran, Terence Conran, Sir Terence Orby Conran)
6 *Titanic*
7 Germany
8 Marzipan
9 The Alps
10 Gladiolus (accept gladioli)
11 Mercury
12 Vulcanisation (accept vulcanizing)
13 Tacking
14 Ned Kelly (accept Edward Kelly)
15 Plymouth
16 A. A. Milne (Alan Alexander Milne)
17 Fox
18 Scottish National Party (accept SNP)
19 Cycling
20 Aldous Huxley

Round 96

1 In the 1991 film *Frankie and Johnny*, who played Frankie alongside Al Pacino?

2 Which aid to medical diagnosis was discovered by Wilhelm Runtgen?

3 What name is given to the barristers' chambers Cherie Blair helped to set up, as well as the name of a 1999 science-fiction film starring Keanu Reeves?

4 What A describes any medication that neutralises stomach acid?

5 In classical music, a piano trio is a chamber ensemble usually consisting of a piano, a violin and what other instrument?

6 Which London Underground station serves both Harrods and Harvey Nichols?

7 Which Scottish singer married Bee Gee Maurice Gibb in 1969?

8 What G is a type of British biscuit, often known as a 'squashed-fly' biscuit?

9 How old was James Dean when he died: 21, 24 or 26?

10 Who wrote 'Verses on the Death of Dr Swift', published in 1739?

11 In the animal kingdom, is a 'hobby' a wader or a falcon?

12 What is the name of the French national anthem?

13 Amnesty International won the Nobel Peace Prize in which decade: the 1960s, 1970s or 1980s?

14 Lisbon is the capital city of which European country?

15 In snooker, which ball has the higher value, brown or green?

16 In biology, does an anaerobic organism need oxygen to survive?

17 In transport, what colour 'cats' eyes' separate the lanes leaving a motorway from the nearside lane?

18 What 1993 film tells the story of a Jamaican bobsleigh team?

19 Is Northern Ireland or Wales larger, in terms of population?

20 To which family of flowering plants does aloe vera belong: the rose or the lily family?

Previous Total

1,000

800

600

450

300

200

100

50

20

0

Banked

Total

Answers

1 Michelle Pfeiffer	**11** Falcon
2 X-rays	**12** 'La Marseillaise'
3 Matrix	**13** 1970s (in 1977)
4 Antacid	**14** Portugal
5 Cello (accept violoncello)	**15** Brown
6 Knightsbridge	**16** No
7 Lulu	**17** Green
8 Garibaldi	**18** Cool Runnings
9 24	**19** Wales
10 [Jonathan] Swift	**20** Lily

Round 97

1 In the musical *West Side Story*, was Riff a member of the Jets or the Sharks?

2 Which country lost football's Euro 2000 final in Holland?

3 In nature, is the monkey puzzle tree a type of conifer?

4 In film, Sir John Gielgud won an Oscar for playing Dudley Moore's butler in which 1981 comedy?

5 In what sport might a player 'snap' the ball to the quarterback?

6 What C is the name given to the white ball in a game of snooker?

7 Mozart's last symphony, number 41, is named after which planet?

8 In the TV series *Friends*, what is the relationship between Monica and Ross?

9 In government, for what do the letters DTI stand?

10 In the animal kingdom, the dogfish belongs to which family of fish?

11 The Chilterns are a notable feature of which English county?

12 The 1993 film *What's Love Got to Do with It?* was about the stormy lives of which married American musical couple?

13 In food, which N is a confection of boiled syrup, beaten egg white, nuts and fruit?

14 Which actor played Travis Bickle in the cult film *Taxi Driver*?

15 In history, the battle of Crécy was the first important land battle of which war fought between 1337 and 1453?

16 In politics, what *S* is a state that has no official ties to any religious movement?

17 Which of these is not an Olympic event: mountain biking, softball or netball?

18 Is the Mojave Desert in the northern or the southern hemisphere?

19 In which European capital city is the train station Tara Street?

20 What nationality is Formula One motor racing champion Michael Schumacker?

Previous Total

1,000

800

600

450

300

200

100

50

20

0

Banked

Total

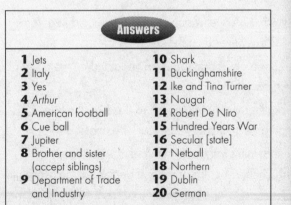

Answers

1 Jets
2 Italy
3 Yes
4 *Arthur*
5 American football
6 Cue ball
7 Jupiter
8 Brother and sister (accept siblings)
9 Department of Trade and Industry
10 Shark
11 Buckinghamshire
12 Ike and Tina Turner
13 Nougat
14 Robert De Niro
15 Hundred Years War
16 Secular [state]
17 Netball
18 Northern
19 Dublin
20 German

1 Which British daily newspaper features the *Fred Bassett* cartoon strip?

2 In which year did the hovercraft cease cross-channel services?

3 In food, 'antipasto' is the Italian term for which course of a meal?

4 Which British athlete won the gold medal in the women's heptathlon at the 2000 Sydney Olympic Games?

5 Which two colours make up the Greek national flag?

6 Which Victorian author wrote the novel *Vanity Fair*, first published in 1847?

7 'Osier' is the name given to twigs from which genus of tree, when used in basket-making?

8 What do the letters FAO stand for when written on a fax?

9 In which 1970s television comedy series did Reg Varney star as bus driver Stan Butler?

10 The Cape of Good Hope is a headland on the coast of which country?

11 In science, which term is used to describe the lowest temperature that can theoretically be attained?

12 Were Britain's first basic state old-age pensions established in the first or second decade of the twentieth century?

13 In human biology, is amblyopia a loss of hearing, sight or taste?

14 Moccasin shoes are part of the traditional costume of which people?

15 What M is used to describe a cinema with a large number of screens?

16 Which Canadian author wrote *Anne of Green Gables*?

17 In which decade was polythene discovered?

18 Which Rogers and Hammerstein musical is named after a fairground attraction?

19 Which creatures would an apiculturist keep?

20 In economics, for what do the letters ERM stand?

Previous Total

1,000

800

600

450

300

200

100

50

20

0

Banked

Total

Answers

1 *Daily Mail* (accept *Mail*/ the *Mail*)

2 2000

3 Starter (accept first course, appetiser, hors d'oeuvres)

4 Denise Lewis

5 Blue and white

6 [William Makepeace] Thackeray

7 Willow (accept *Salix* or *Salicaceae*)

8 For the attention of (accept for attention of)

9 *On the Buses*

10 South Africa

11 Absolute zero

12 First (1900s) (Old Age Pensions Act 1908)

13 Sight

14 [North] American Indians/ Native Americans (accept Amerindian(s); accept Red Indian, but may be regarded as offensive)

15 Multiplex

16 Lucy Maud Montgomery (accept L M Montgomery)

17 1930s

18 *Carousel*

19 Bees

20 Exchange Rate

Round 99

1 The film *Quadrophenia* was based on which rock band's best-selling album?

2 In human biology, which is longer: the large or small intestine?

3 Which Hollywood actress starred in Steven Spielberg's *ET* when she was only seven years old?

4 In geography, how many continental landmasses lie entirely in the southern hemisphere?

5 In 1707, did the Act of Union unite England with Scotland or Wales?

6 Which Australian film actress starred in the West End production of *The Blue Room* in 1998?

7 The Egyptian plover is a bird reputed to pick decayed food and grubs from the mouth of which creature?

8 In what 1960s US sitcom did Jed Clampett strike oil and move his family from the country to the city?

9 In theatre, which nineteenth-century Norwegian playwright wrote the drama *Peer Gynt*?

10 What nationality is the operatic tenor José Carreras?

11 In Britain, which day marks the start of the grouse-shooting season?

12 In fashion, is a baggy sweater known as a Sloppy Joe or a Sloppy Jim?

13 In geography, in which country is the city of Casablanca?

14 The name of which Italian politician and author, born in 1469, is synonymous with amoral cunning?

15 In which *Lethal Weapon* film did Patsy Kensit star as Mel Gibson's love interest?

16 In humans, what specific part of the body is affected by an embolism?

17 'Shall We Dance?' is a song from which Rodgers and Hammerstein musical?

18 What A is a trinket or jewel worn as a protection against evil?

19 In maths, add the number of Snow White's dwarfs to the number of degrees in a right angle.

20 What was the name of Frank Spencer's wife in the 1970s sitcom *Some Mothers Do 'Ave 'Em*?

Previous Total

1,000

800

600

450

300

200

100

50

20

0

Banked

Total

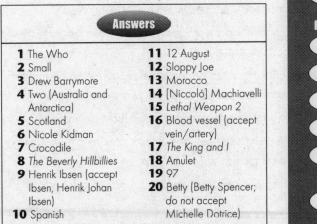

Answers

1 The Who
2 Small
3 Drew Barrymore
4 Two (Australia and Antarctica)
5 Scotland
6 Nicole Kidman
7 Crocodile
8 *The Beverly Hillbillies*
9 Henrik Ibsen (accept Ibsen, Henrik Johan Ibsen)
10 Spanish
11 12 August
12 Sloppy Joe
13 Morocco
14 [Niccoló] Machiavelli
15 *Lethal Weapon 2*
16 Blood vessel (accept vein/artery)
17 *The King and I*
18 Amulet
19 97
20 Betty (Betty Spencer; do not accept Michelle Dotrice)

Round 100

1 What is the name of the palace in Woodstock Park near Oxford?

2 How were the Chinese forced to wear their hair by their Manchu conquerors until 1912?

3 Is Papua New Guinea situated directly north of Australia or New Zealand?

4 In theatre, which venue is the London home of the Royal Shakespeare Company?

5 In pop music, sisters Nicole and Nathalie Appleton are members of which girl group?

6 In mythology, which time of day is the Greek goddess Eos said to personify?

7 In nature, does the larch tree keep or lose its needles during the winter?

8 In history, in which year did South Yemen declare its independence from the British: 1947 or 1967?

9 In humans, arteriography is the X-ray examination of what part of the body?

10 In cooking, what *F* can be described as 'an open pastry or sponge case containing a sweet or savoury filling'?

11 In what sport do players contest rucks and mauls?

12 Approximately how long does it take the planet Jupiter to orbit the sun once: five years or twelve years?

13 In the 1997 film *Men In Black*, who played Agent J?

14 Which animal's male and female are called 'jack' and 'jenny'?

15 In what 1960s television cowboy series did Clint Eastwood star as Rowdy Yates alongside Eric Fleming as Gil Favor?

16 Which religious movement was founded in the USA in 1830 by Joseph Smith?

17 In football, which was the first British club to win the European Cup?

18 Oxford University and the Royal Engineers were winners of what competition in 1874 and 1875 respectively?

19 The Union Jack flag combines the crosses of three saints: George, Andrew and whom?

20 In classical music, which Italian composer wrote the opera *La Traviata* in 1853?

Previous Total

1,000

800

600

450

300

200

100

50

20

0

Banked

Total

Answers

1 Blenheim
2 In a pigtail (accept in a 'queue')
3 Australia
4 The Barbican Centre (accept Barbican)
5 All Saints
6 Dawn
7 Loses its needles
8 1967
9 Arteries (accept blood vessels)
10 Flan
11 Rugby Union (*not* League)

12 Twelve years
13 Will Smith
14 Ass, or donkey (accept mule)
15 *Rawhide*
16 Mormonism (accept the Mormons/The Church of Jesus Christ of Latter-day Saints)
17 Celtic (accept Glasgow Celtic)
18 The FA Cup (accept FA Challenge Cup)
19 Patrick
20 [Giuseppe] Verdi

Round 101

1 In which English county would you find the town of Bury St Edmunds?

2 How many seats does a tandem usually have?

3 In the animal kingdom, is it the male or the female mosquito that usually requires a blood meal?

4 In sport, how many track and field events make up the heptathlon?

5 In clothing, what V is the American term for a waistcoat?

6 In music, 'Brown Eyed Girl' and 'Bright Side of the Road' were hits for which Belfast-born singer-songwriter?

7 In geography, in which country are the cities of Edmonton, Winnipeg, Thunder Bay and Calgary?

8 In athletics, who won the 100 m gold at the 2000 Sydney Olympic Games: Dwaine Chambers or Maurice Greene?

9 What A is the scientific study of mankind?

10 Lending its name to one of his poems, in which jail was Oscar Wilde imprisoned?

11 In geography, in which US state would you find the Everglades National Park?

12 What musical instrument does astronomer Patrick Moore sometimes play on television?

13 Complete the title of the Thomas Hardy novel of 1886: The Mayor of . . .?

14 In ancient Egypt, which *P* were worshipped as kings and gods?

15 In nature, what name is usually given to the flowers of apple and cherry trees?

16 On which US television cartoon series did Dick Dastardly race against Penelope Pitstop and the Ant Hill Mob?

17 In which English county would you find the town of Whitstable?

18 What was the full name of Han Solo's big hairy friend in *Star Wars*?

19 How many natural satellites orbit the planet Earth?

20 Which cricket team won the English County Championship in September 2000?

Previous Total

1,000
800
600
450
300
200
100
50
20
0

Banked

Total

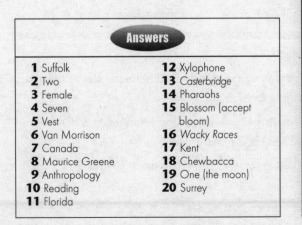

Answers

1 Suffolk	**12** Xylophone
2 Two	**13** *Casterbridge*
3 Female	**14** Pharaohs
4 Seven	**15** Blossom (accept
5 Vest	bloom)
6 Van Morrison	**16** *Wacky Races*
7 Canada	**17** Kent
8 Maurice Greene	**18** Chewbacca
9 Anthropology	**19** One (the moon)
10 Reading	**20** Surrey
11 Florida	

Round 102

1 Name George Orwell's 1945 novel which satirises revolutionary Russia in events on a farm.

2 In maths, what is 19 multiplied by 4?

3 King George VI became heir to the throne when who abdicated in 1936?

4 In the animal kingdom, is the opossum of North America a marsupial or a rodent?

5 In which country of the UK is the Forth Bridge?

6 What blasting explosive was patented in 1867 by Alfred Nobel?

7 In history, which East European country was invaded by the Germans on 1 September 1939?

8 Proverbially, a cat has how many lives?

9 Complete the name of this country in the West Indies: Trinidad and . . . what?

10 What is the name of Sir Thomas More's book of 1516 about a fictional country where everything seemed to be perfect?

11 What *F* is a type of laminated plastic material often used for table tops?

12 In film, Arnold Schwarzenegger starred as a barbarian in which 1982 fantasy film?

13 Who is married to comedian Lenny Henry?

14 In cooking, what *F* is a chewy biscuit made of oats, sugar, butter and golden syrup?

15 In pop music, who was the lead singer of the Scottish band Wet Wet Wet?

16 In geography, is Angola on the east or west coast of Africa?

17 In nature, what *T* is a common herbaceous plant of the daisy family, typically with a prickly stem and leaves?

18 What substance, forming part of the human tooth, is the hardest substance in the human body?

19 In the life cycle of a star, which comes first, a white dwarf or a black dwarf?

20 Simon Groom, John Leslie and Lesley Judd all presented which long-running children's television show?

Previous Total

1,000
800
600
450
300
200
100
50
20
0

Banked

Total

Answers

1 *Animal Farm*
2 76
3 Edward VIII (do *not* accept Duke of Windsor)
4 Marsupial
5 Scotland
6 Dynamite
7 Poland
8 Nine
9 Tobago
10 *Utopia*
11 Formica
12 *Conan the Barbarian*
13 Dawn French
14 Flapjack
15 Marti Pellow
16 West coast
17 Thistle
18 Enamel
19 White dwarf
20 *Blue Peter*

Round 103

1 In theatre, which British novelist and playwright wrote *An Inspector Calls*, published in 1946?

2 Which former Bucks Fizz member became a television presenter on shows including *Record Breakers*?

3 In the New Testament, which disciple was the brother of Simon Peter?

4 Which controversial film by Stanley Kubrick was adapted from an Anthony Burgess novel and starred Malcolm McDowell?

5 In biology, aplastic, pernicious and sickle-cell are all forms of which medical condition?

6 In art, what was the nationality of surrealist painter René Magritte?

7 In which fictional hospital is the television series *Casualty* set?

8 In science, is an alkaloid an organic or inorganic substance?

9 Which London landmark was designed by Sir Norman Foster to depict a 'blade of light by night'?

10 Which jazz trumpeter and composer released the album entitled *Kind of Blue* in 1959?

11 In which Sussex coastal resort is there an area of streets known as The Lanes that is renowned for its antique shops?

12 What B is a jellied dessert whose name comes from the French for 'white food'?

13 The musical *Mamma Mia* is based on the songs of which group?

14 In history, the 1939 'Pact of Steel' was a military alliance between Germany and which other country?

15 Kate Hannigan, Katie Mulholland and Tilly Trotter are all heroines created by which best-selling novelist?

16 In Britain, is it the male or female cuckoo which makes the distinctive 'cuckoo' call?

17 Complete the next line of this nursery rhyme: 'Twinkle, twinkle, little star . . .'

18 In 1911, did Roald Armundsen beat Captain Robert Scott to the North or South Pole?

19 In politics, who became Secretary-General of the United Nations in 1996?

20 Stockholm is the capital city of which European country?

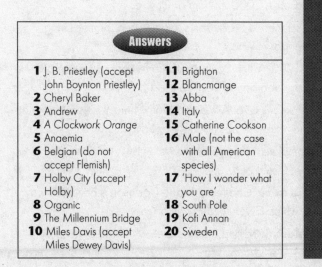

Previous Total

1,000

800

600

450

300

200

100

50

20

0

Banked

Total

Answers

1 J. B. Priestley (accept John Boynton Priestley)
2 Cheryl Baker
3 Andrew
4 *A Clockwork Orange*
5 Anaemia
6 Belgian (do not accept Flemish)
7 Holby City (accept Holby)
8 Organic
9 The Millennium Bridge
10 Miles Davis (accept Miles Dewey Davis)

11 Brighton
12 Blancmange
13 Abba
14 Italy
15 Catherine Cookson
16 Male (not the case with all American species)
17 'How I wonder what you are'
18 South Pole
19 Kofi Annan
20 Sweden

Round 104

1 In nature, *Helianthus* is the botanical name for which flower, grown for its oil?

2 In a French restaurant, what does '*plat du jour*' translate to in English?

3 In television, in which 1960s science fiction show would a robot warn the Robinson family of impending danger?

4 In medicine, what *A* is the name given to a substance that counteracts a poison?

5 What nationality was the film and theatre actress Mae West?

6 Which trio had a massive hit with a cover of Bob Dylan's 'Blowin' in the Wind' in 1963?

7 Which football team got within two wins of Reading's record of thirteen wins from the start of a football league season in 2000, Fulham or Chelsea?

8 In science, a Stevenson screen is used for measuring changes in what?

9 In 1990, which South African president committed himself to the abolition of the apartheid policy?

10 In humans what *A* is a condition where a person's normal body pigment has not developed?

11 Complete the name of this well-known Italian fashion duo: Dolce and . . .?

12 In literature, Charles Lutwidge Dodgson is better known as which Cheshire-born author?

13 Helium, neon and argon are all what kind of gases?

14 In the *Iliad*, who is the god of the dead who Herakles shoots in the shoulder with an arrow?

15 In music, was British singer Lisa Stansfield born in Rochdale or Rotherham?

16 In food, what type of orange is the Seville: sweet or bitter?

17 The song 'Bachelor Boy' comes from which Cliff Richard film?

18 In history, which king was the father of Queen Elizabeth II?

19 In which year did Margaret Thatcher become the leader of the Conservative Party?

20 How many gold medals did Australian swimmer Ian Thorpe win at the Sydney 2000 Olympics?

Previous Total

1,000
800
600
450
300
200
100
50
20
0

Banked

Total

Answers

1 Sunflower
2 Dish of the day
3 *Lost in Space*
4 Antidote
5 American
6 Peter, Paul & Mary
7 Fulham
8 Weather (accept temperature, humidity)
9 F. W. de Klerk (accept Frederik Willem de Klerk)
10 Albino/albinism
11 Gabbana (usually known as Dolce e Gabbana)
12 Lewis Carroll
13 Noble (accept inert)
14 Hades
15 Rochdale
16 Bitter
17 *Summer Holiday*
18 George VI
19 1975
20 Three

1 In which state was President J. F. Kennedy assassinated?

2 Which 1973 Elton John pop song, about Marilyn Monroe, was rewritten in 1997 for the funeral of Diana, Princess of Wales?

3 In the management of aircraft arrivals and departures, ATC stands for what?

4 The Greek national flag consists of how many colours?

5 In literature, John Bunyan is best known for his religious work *The Pilgrim's . . .* what?

6 On the internet or in business, for what do the letters FYI stand on a communication?

7 In the television series, who was private detective Randall's deceased partner, played by Kenneth Cope and later Vic Reeves?

8 In the animal kingdom, are percheron and Andalucian European breeds of horse or cow?

9 Which African country lies the furthest east?

10 In botany, the bluebell is a name commonly used in England and Wales to refer to bulbous perennials belonging to which family of flowers?

11 Which 1979 science fiction film was advertised by the slogan 'In space no one can hear you scream'?

12 In what sport do you have 'slam dunks' and 'lay ups'?

13 What S is a type of poem, favoured by Shakespeare, Milton and Wordsworth, consisting of 14 lines?

14 Which Hollywood child star of the 1990s *Home Alone* films is godfather to Michael Jackson's first child?

15 Which of Puccini's operas is set in Japan?

16 In snooker, what is the total number of balls on the table at the start of a game?

17 In government, for what do the letters DSS stand?

18 'Look at Me, I'm Sandra Dee' is a song from which stage and screen musical?

19 In nature, two types of tree dominate the European deciduous forests: beech and which other?

20 In health, which organisation is usually known by the initials WHO?

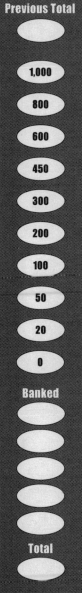

Previous Total

1,000
800
600
450
300
200
100
50
20
0

Banked

Total

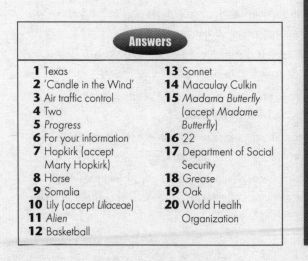

Answers

1 Texas
2 'Candle in the Wind'
3 Air traffic control
4 Two
5 Progress
6 For your information
7 Hopkirk (accept Marty Hopkirk)
8 Horse
9 Somalia
10 Lily (accept *Liliaceae*)
11 *Alien*
12 Basketball
13 Sonnet
14 Macaulay Culkin
15 *Madama Butterfly* (accept *Madame Butterfly*)
16 22
17 Department of Social Security
18 *Grease*
19 Oak
20 World Health Organization

Round 106

1 The musical *Oliver!* is based on a novel by which author?

2 Which extinct relative of the elephant lived in every continent except Australia and South America?

3 In pop music, what was the name of the first album by Oasis?

4 In humans, what is the opposite of the medical condition acidosis?

5 In a 1999 poll carried out by the British Association of Toy Retailers, what small toy was voted the Craze of the Century?

6 From which country did Albania win independence in 1912?

7 In what year was the British voting age reduced to eighteen: 1967 or 1970?

8 Which American jazz trumpeter and singer was known by the nickname 'Satchmo'?

9 Which *S* is a three-leafed plant, said to have been used by St Patrick to represent the Holy Trinity?

10 In children's stories, what overweight schoolboy attended Greyfriars School?

11 In the Shakespeare play *Romeo and Juliet*, was Juliet's surname Montague or Capulet?

12 Which twentieth-century artist's work includes *The Persistence of Memory*, *Crucifixion*, and *The Sacrament of the Last Supper*?

13 Name the female athlete from South Africa who was given British citizenship in order to compete in the 1984 Olympic Games?

14 Is the name Lalique associated with glass or ceramics?

15 What is the name of the central banking authority of the USA?

16 Charles I's rejection of Parliament's Nineteen Propositions led to the beginning of which war?

17 In the Bible, which *D* was Solomon's father?

18 Which was the first *Star Trek* film to feature Captain Picard?

19 In females, labour pains are caused by the contractions of which internal organ?

20 In which country is the musical *Fiddler on the Roof* set?

Previous Total

1,000

800

600

450

300

200

100

50

20

0

Banked

Total

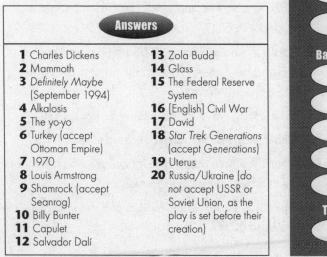

Answers

1 Charles Dickens
2 Mammoth
3 *Definitely Maybe* (September 1994)
4 Alkalosis
5 The yo-yo
6 Turkey (accept Ottoman Empire)
7 1970
8 Louis Armstrong
9 Shamrock (accept Seanrog)
10 Billy Bunter
11 Capulet
12 Salvador Dalí

13 Zola Budd
14 Glass
15 The Federal Reserve System
16 [English] Civil War
17 David
18 *Star Trek Generations* (accept *Generations*)
19 Uterus
20 Russia/Ukraine (do *not* accept USSR or Soviet Union, as the play is set before their creation)

Round 107

1 In America, Paul Revere's house is a feature of which Massachusetts city?

2 What G is an English artist born in 1727 who is famous for his landscapes and portraits?

3 In medicine, is an aneurysm a weak spot in a vein or an artery?

4 In which decade did the musical *Cats* open in London?

5 Britain's first canal, the Bridgewater, was built to transport which fuel?

6 Are puffins a type of penguin or a type of ork?

7 Which European city is home to Olsens' World Clock?

8 In theatre, which Peter was born in 1921 and starred in his own play of 1956, *Romanoff and Juliet*?

9 Ronan Keating became famous as the lead singer with which pop group?

10 In politics, whose election as US president in 1860 triggered the protests of the southern states before the American Civil War?

11 In mythology, was Achilles a Greek or Roman hero?

12 What F includes mushrooms, yeasts and moulds?

13 What is the more usual name for the air-cushion machine invented by Christopher Cockerell?

14 Which woman was prime minister of Israel between 1969 and 1974?

15 In humans, what name is given to the cord that connects an unborn infant to the placenta?

16 In food, ascorbic acid is also known as what vitamin?

17 In what sport do you find the teams the London Wasps and the Sale Sharks?

18 What was the name of the spacecraft that famously penetrated the head of Halley's Comet in 1986?

19 In which film does Julia Roberts's character fake her own death to escape domestic violence?

20 In the animal kingdom, to which family of reptiles do caymans belong?

Previous Total

1,000
800
600
450
300
200
100
50
20
0

Banked

Total

Answers

1 Boston
2 Gainsborough (accept Thomas Gainsborough)
3 Artery
4 1980s (1981)
5 Coal
6 Ork
7 Copenhagen
8 [Peter] Ustinov
9 Boyzone
10 Abraham Lincoln
11 Greek
12 Fungus
13 Hovercraft

14 [Mrs] Golda Meir
15 Umbilical cord (accept umbilicus)
16 [Vitamin] C
17 Rugby Union (accept Rugby; do not accept Rugby League)
18 Giotto
19 Sleeping with the Enemy
20 Crocodile (accept alligator)

Round 108

1 Which rock star has appeared in the films *The Man Who Fell to Earth* and *Merry Christmas Mr Lawrence*?

2 What nationality was Karen Blixen, the author of *Out of Africa*, Danish or American?

3 How many colours are there on a Rubik's Cube?

4 Countess Markiewicz, Britain's first elected woman MP, refused to take her seat. For which political party was she elected?

5 In our solar system, is the planet Venus or the planet Earth closer to the sun?

6 What name is given to the milky fluid exuded by the rubber tree?

7 In the Bible, who was swallowed by a 'great fish'?

8 *Hippocampus hippocampus* is the scientific name for which sea creature, the sea horse or the starfish?

9 In which London arts complex is the National Theatre?

10 In America, the George Washington Bridge crosses the Hudson River in which state?

11 Which unit of power, often used to express the rate of work of an engine, was devised by James Watt?

12 Which writer, creator of Jeeves, got into hot water for a series of wartime broadcasts from Germany?

13 What was James Dean's last film?

14 In sport, French World Cup goalkeeper Fabien Barthez joined which English football team in 2000?

15 Waikiki Beach is a resort in which American state?

16 In carpentry, the 'claw' and 'ball pein' are both types of which tool?

17 Which UK politician has been referred to by the tabloids as 'Two Jags'?

18 In which year was VAT introduced in Britain?

19 Whose is the first death recounted in the Bible?

20 In medicine, what name is given to the yellowing of the skin caused by a build-up of bile pigments in the blood?

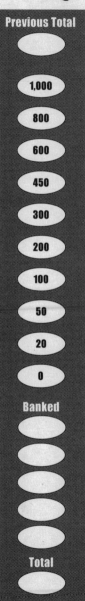

Previous Total

1,000

800

600

450

300

200

100

50

20

0

Banked

Total

Answers

1 David Bowie	**12** P. G. Wodehouse
2 Danish	(accept Sir Palham
3 Six	Granville
4 Sinn Fein	Wodehouse)
5 Venus	**13** Giant
6 Latex	**14** Manchester United
7 Jonah	**15** Hawaii
8 Sea horse	**16** Hammer
9 The South Bank	**17** John Prescott (accept
Centre (accept the	deputy prime minister)
South Bank)	**18** 1973
10 New York	**19** Abel's
11 Horsepower	**20** Jaundice

Round 109

1 Which English author wrote *Our Man in Havana* and *Brighton Rock*?

2 How many metres make up one kilometre?

3 Which overture by Tchaikovsky incorporates the 'Marseillaise' and is still sometimes performed with a cannon and bells?

4 Which castle is the main home of the Duke of Northumberland?

5 In nature, what colour are the flowers of the shrub *Forsythia*?

6 'Border Leicester' and 'blackface' are breeds of which farm animal?

7 Which comic-book superhero is described as 'faster than a speeding bullet, more powerful than a locomotive'?

8 What S describes a low marshland that is permanently wet?

9 Was American artist John Singer Sargent famed for his portraits or landscapes?

10 Name the former pop group made up of George Michael and Andrew Ridgeley.

11 The annual veteran car rally runs between London and which south-coast town?

12 Lord Reith was the first and Greg Dyke is the latest director general of which organisation?

13 The certificate from an employer showing earnings and tax deducted during a complete tax year is known as a 'P . . .' what?

14 In which country is the African National Congress the ruling political party?

15 In astrology, which star sign falls between the star signs of Cancer and Virgo?

16 In architecture, are Norman arches rounded or pointed?

17 Which human rights organisation was awarded the Nobel Peace Prize in 1977?

18 What M is the name given to a document issued by a political party at election time, setting out its programme for government?

19 Abruzzi is a mountainous region of which European country?

20 In the Bible, who was the first person to eat from the Tree of Knowledge of good and evil?

Previous Total

1,000
800
600
450
300
200
100
50
20
0

Banked

Total

Answers

1 Graham Greene	**12** The BBC, or British
2 1000 metres	Broadcasting
3 1812 Overture	Corporation
4 Alnwick	**13** [P]60
5 Yellow	**14** South Africa
6 Sheep	**15** Leo
7 Superman	**16** Rounded
8 Swamp	**17** Amnesty International
9 Portraits	**18** Manifesto
10 Wham!	**19** Italy
11 Brighton	**20** Eve

Round 110

1 Spice Girl Mel B's daughter shares her name with which mythical creature?

2 Which M is a common alternative name for the peanut?

3 What was the name of the 1960s model known as 'The Shrimp'?

4 In sport, Zimbabwe and which other test cricket team toured England in the summer of 2000?

5 Emma Samms played the character Fallon in which 1980s television soap opera, which was a spin-off from *Dynasty*?

6 What does VJ Day commemorate?

7 In the New Testament, who is named as the author of the letter to the Galatians?

8 What is basketball player Magic Johnson's real first name?

9 Beirut is the capital city of which country?

10 In geography, the St Lawrence River connects the Great Lakes to which ocean?

11 What is the meaning of the musical term 'fortissimo'?

12 Which US president was shot in 1865?

13 In which sport might a 'bridge' and a 'rack' be used?

14 In the American television series of the 1960s and 1970s, what was the family name of the Beverly Hillbillies?

15 The SNCF is the national railway system of which country?

16 In imperial weights, 28 pounds is equivalent to how many stones?

17 2.47 acres is the imperial equivalent of how many hectares?

18 Now a director, who, as a young actor, co-starred with his wife Sheila Sim in the original theatre production of *The Mousetrap* in 1952?

19 In pop music, which Frankie Goes To Hollywood song was reportedly banned by the BBC in 1984?

20 The capital city Jakarta is found on which Indonesian island?

Previous Total

1,000

800

600

450

300

200

100

50

20

0

Banked

Total

Answers

1 Phoenix
2 Monkey nut
3 Jean Shrimpton
4 West Indies
5 *The Colbys*
6 Victory over Japan (accept the end of World War II)
7 Paul (St Paul the Apostle)
8 Earvin
9 [Republic of] Lebanon
10 [North] Atlantic
11 Very loud (accept very strong)
12 Abraham Lincoln
13 Snooker/billiards/pool
14 The Clampetts
15 France
16 Two
17 One
18 Richard Attenborough (Lord Richard Samuel Attenborough)
19 'Relax'
20 Java

Round 111

1 In English law, what name is given to the crime of marrying while still legally married to someone else?

2 The city of Carlisle in Cumbria lies on which river?

3 In which country was the British television soap *Eldorado* set?

4 In the New Testament, who was beheaded at the request of the daughter of Herodias?

5 Which car company produced a model called the Testarossa?

6 In food, which fruit is the basis of the dish 'guacamole'?

7 Which sign of the zodiac is represented by a member of the cat family?

8 In the television programme *EastEnders*, the di Marco family left Albert Square to live in which county?

9 In which decade did Brighton become Britain's first town or city to have permanent electric street lighting?

10 In the *Star Wars* films, who does the young Anakin Skywalker grow up to become?

11 In which country is Tel Aviv?

12 Prince William left which school in 2000 after completing his A levels?

13 In which month is the Queen and Prince Philip's wedding anniversary?

14 Which 1995 John Grisham novel was made into a film directed by Francis Ford Coppola?

15 In pop music, *Waking Up the Neighbours* and *So Far So Good* are albums by which Canadian singer and songwriter?

16 With what sport would you primarily associate Jeremy Guscott?

17 What nationality is the famous fashion designer Givenchy?

18 Complete the title of the James Joyce novel, *A Portrait of the Artist as a . . .* what?

19 In the animal kingdom, how many humps does an Arabian camel have?

20 Was the Greek philosopher Aristotle born AD or BC?

Previous Total

1,000

800

600

450

300

200

100

50

20

0

Banked

Total

Answers

1 Bigamy (*do not accept polygamy*)
2 Eden
3 Spain
4 John the Baptist (accept the Forerunner)
5 Ferrari
6 Avocado
7 Leo (the lion)
8 Leicestershire
9 1880s (1882)
10 Darth Vader
11 Israel
12 Eton College (accept Eton)
13 November
14 *The Rainmaker*
15 Bryan Adams
16 Rugby [Union]
17 French
18 *Young Man*
19 One
20 BC (born 384 BC)

Round 112

1 How many kilograms make up one metric tonne?

2 In fashion, what type of garment is a 'cloche'?

3 'Tamworth' and 'Berkshire' are both breeds of which farm animal?

4 Does the city of Carlisle lie on the eastern or western end of Hadrian's Wall?

5 Which painter immortalised the dancer Jane Avril in posters for the Moulin Rouge?

6 In Britain, can an unaccompanied eleven-year-old legally buy a pet?

7 Which English football team had a UK Top 10 chart hit with 'Blue is the Colour' in 1972?

8 In food, which pulse forms the basis of the Greek dish hummus?

9 In the animal kingdom, the 'yucca' is a species of which insect?

10 Which city in the English Midlands is served by New Street station?

11 In education, which letter represents the lowest-grade pass in GCSE exams?

12 In pop music, 'Millennium' was a hit for which former member of Take That?

13 In film, who played the Spice Girls' manager in *SpiceWorld: The Movie*?

14 In dressmaking, featherweight, skirt weight, and open-ended are all types of what?

15 The Bridgewater Hall in Manchester is the home of which orchestra?

16 In literature, the author Isabel Allende is from which South American country?

17 In the Gregorian calendar, how many months of the year have thirty days in them?

18 Which ocean lies between the Americas and Asia?

19 The actor Michael Caine is said to have used which film as the inspiration for his stage name?

20 What is the official language of Sardinia?

Previous Total

1,000
800
600
450
300
200
100
50
20
0

Banked

Total

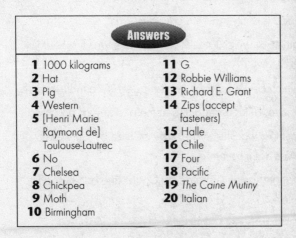

Answers

1 1000 kilograms
2 Hat
3 Pig
4 Western
5 [Henri Marie Raymond de] Toulouse-Lautrec
6 No
7 Chelsea
8 Chickpea
9 Moth
10 Birmingham
11 G
12 Robbie Williams
13 Richard E. Grant
14 Zips (accept fasteners)
15 Halle
16 Chile
17 Four
18 Pacific
19 *The Caine Mutiny*
20 Italian

Round 113

1 In which month is the birthday of the present Duke of York?

2 In the animal kingdom, where does the male Darwin's frog carry his mate's eggs until they have developed into tiny frogs?

3 In music, which rap star's real name is Marshall Mathers?

4 With which sport would you associate David Campese?

5 Complete the title of this Wham! pop song: 'Wake Me Up Before You . . . ' what?

6 In children's literature, which girl famously lives at Green Gables?

7 On English television, who presents *Auntie's Bloomers* and *Auntie's Sporting Bloomers*?

8 Which English spa town, famous since Roman times, is the home of the famous Georgian Royal Crescent?

9 Genoa is a city in which country?

10 In athletics, which famous London race was first held in 1981?

11 In which century did the English poet William Blake die?

12 In nature, is 'jacaranda' the name of a tree or an animal?

13 In fashion, was the 'A-line' style created by Christian Dior or Yves Saint Laurent?

14 What profession is shared by Carla Lane and Lynda La Plante?

15 Who won the Spanish Civil War in 1939: the Republicans or the Nationalists?

16 In the children's rhyme, what animal did Tom the piper's son steal?

17 What was the third channel to appear on British television?

18 In medicine, what part of the abdomen would be inflamed if you had the disorder colitis?

19 Which former prime minister took his name from Rievaulx Abbey on his elevation to the peerage in 1983, Harold Wilson or James Callaghan?

20 In pop music, who duetted with Aretha Franklin on the number one hit 'I Knew You Were Waiting for Me'?

Previous Total

1,000

800

600

450

300

200

100

50

20

0

Banked

Total

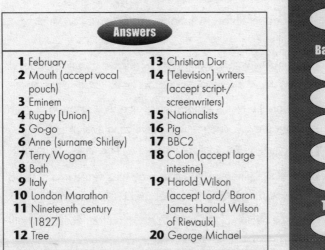

Answers

1 February
2 Mouth (accept vocal pouch)
3 Eminem
4 Rugby [Union]
5 Go-go
6 Anne (surname Shirley)
7 Terry Wogan
8 Bath
9 Italy
10 London Marathon
11 Nineteenth century (1827)
12 Tree
13 Christian Dior
14 [Television] writers (accept script-/ screenwriters)
15 Nationalists
16 Pig
17 BBC2
18 Colon (accept large intestine)
19 Harold Wilson (accept Lord/ Baron James Harold Wilson of Rievaulx)
20 George Michael

Round 114

1 Which Hollywood star was born Archibald Leach in Bristol in 1904?

2 How were the authors Lawrence Durrell and Gerald Durrell related?

3 In the animal kingdom, the mandrill is an ape native to which continent?

4 In the nursery rhyme, what was Wee Willie Winkie wearing as he ran through the town?

5 'Girls Just Want to Have Fun' was which singer's debut single?

6 Traditionally, the sweet pea is a birth flower associated with which month?

7 Which Emily Brontë novel was made into a film in 1939 starring Laurence Olivier?

8 In ancient history, Memphis was a capital of which country?

9 In maths, which chart, to show relative quantities, consists of a circle divided into appropriately sized segments?

10 Before he hit the big screen, Bruce Willis starred opposite Cybill Shepherd in which television series?

11 In which Russian city is the famous Hermitage museum?

12 Which Tennessee Williams play was made into a 1958 film starring Elizabeth Taylor and Paul Newman?

13 In the human body, ossification is the formation of what?

14 Which comedian hosted the year 2000's Academy Awards Ceremony?

15 The orbit of which planet lies between those of Earth and Mercury?

16 In nature, what part of a fly generates the buzzing sound?

17 In which English naval city does The Hoe overlook The Sound?

18 What is the usual French translation for the English word 'milk'?

19 What nationality is the Nobel Prize-winning author Günter Grass?

20 Which 1985 John Irving novel was made into a film starring Michael Caine?

Previous Total

1,000

800

600

450

300

200

100

50

20

0

Banked

Total

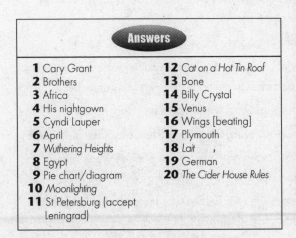

Answers

1 Cary Grant
2 Brothers
3 Africa
4 His nightgown
5 Cyndi Lauper
6 April
7 *Wuthering Heights*
8 Egypt
9 Pie chart/diagram
10 *Moonlighting*
11 St Petersburg (accept Leningrad)

12 *Cat on a Hot Tin Roof*
13 Bone
14 Billy Crystal
15 Venus
16 Wings [beating]
17 Plymouth
18 *Lait*
19 German
20 *The Cider House Rules*

1 On which body of water does the French resort Biarritz lie?

2 In the animal kingdom, which has more legs, a lobster or a scorpion?

3 Traditionally, in Britain, the chrysanthemum is a flower associated with which month?

4 In physics, what is the minimum number of metals needed to form an alloy?

5 In physics, what unit of electromotive force was named after Count Alessandro Volta?

6 Which planet has been called both 'the morning star' and 'the evening star'?

7 Followers of which religion face towards Mecca to pray?

8 In geology, what A is the most abundant metal in the crust of the Earth?

9 In mobile phones, for what does 'WAP' stand?

10 In which decade did British weather reports start giving temperatures in centigrade as well as Fahrenheit?

11 In clothing, what would spats be attached to?

12 In the nursery rhyme, who made Cock Robin's shroud?

13 Pre-decimalisation, how many pennies were there in a pound sterling?

14 In television, Cliff Barnes was the arch-enemy of which 1980s soap character?

15 Which independent nation in the West Indies is the most easterly of the Caribbean islands?

16 In the game of draughts, how many pieces are there on the board at the beginning of a game?

17 The American television series *Chicago Hope* is set in which type of establishment?

18 How many counties make up Northern Ireland?

19 In sport, which country won the women's Olympic team gold in gymnastics in every games from 1952 to 1980?

20 Which jazz singer is married to Johnny Dankworth?

Previous Total

1,000

800

600

450

300

200

100

50

20

0

Banked

Total

Answers

1 Atlantic Ocean (accept Bay of Biscay)
2 Lobster (has ten legs; scorpion has eight)
3 November
4 Two
5 The volt
6 Venus
7 Islam/Muslims
8 Aluminium
9 Wireless Application Protocol
10 1960s (1962)
11 Shoes/boots/footwear
12 The beetle
13 240
14 J. R. Ewing (accept J. R.)
15 Barbados
16 24
17 Hospital
18 Six
19 Soviet Union (accept USSR, Russia)
20 Cleo Laine

Round 116

1 In the television comedy series *Porridge*, what was the name of Fletcher's regular cellmate?

2 'The Angel of the North' statue towers above which A-road near Gateshead?

3 In which country would you find the city of Sarajevo?

4 In what century were the Blackpool illuminations lit up for the first time?

5 Which Scottish city is the home of the Kelvingrove Art Gallery?

6 How many female prime ministers of the United Kingdom have there been?

7 In geology, is the rare mineral Blue John mined in Cornwall or in Derbyshire?

8 Who presented the 'Britain's Strongest Man' competition for the BBC in the year 2000?

9 What *V* is the country with the highest cable-car system in the world?

10 In pop music, which Irish family group released the album *Talk On Corners*?

11 What was the name of the ship on which explorer Christopher Columbus set sail in 1492?

12 What *D* is a hard rock that shares a name with a range of North Italian mountains?

13 Which animal belongs to the 'pinnipeds' family, a bat or a seal?

14 In the Beatrix Potter story, what is Mrs Tiggywinkle's profession?

15 In which Yorkshire city was the artist David Hockney born?

16 Gamal Nasser and Anwar Sadat were both leaders of which Middle Eastern country?

17 Which pop band's 1994 debut album was *Definitely Maybe*?

18 Traditionally, in the UK, the carnation is a birth flower associated with which month?

19 In which decade did wearing seatbelts in the back of the car become compulsory for adults?

20 Which car, designed by Alec Issigonis for the British Motor Corporation, was launched in 1959?

Previous Total

1,000

800

600

450

300

200

100

50

20

0

Banked

Total

Answers

1 [Lennie] Godber
2 A1 (do not accept A1 (M))
3 Bosnia-Hercegovina (accept Bosnia)
4 Nineteenth
5 Glasgow
6 One
7 Derbyshire (Peak District)
8 John Inverdale
9 Venezuela
10 The Corrs
11 *Santa Maria*
12 Dolomite
13 Seal
14 Laundress (accept takes in washing, washerwoman)
15 Bradford
16 Egypt
17 Oasis
18 January
19 1990s (1991)
20 Mini

Round 117

1 With which type of television programme was Geoff Hamilton primarily associated?

2 The 'Cross of Lorraine', adopted as their symbol by the Free French during World War II, has how many horizontal bars?

3 Which Dutch painter, usually known only by his first name, had the surname van Rijn?

4 Where on the body would a cravat normally be worn?

5 In which subject does one encounter sines, cosines and tangents?

6 Which architect designed the Sagrada Familia cathedral in Barcelona?

7 The outside of the Statue of Liberty is made from which metal?

8 In pop music, René Angelil is the manager and husband of which French-Canadian singer?

9 Who directed the films *North by Northwest* and *Vertigo*?

10 In the animal kingdom, the 'Kodiak' is the largest Alaskan variety of which carnivore?

11 In the international phonetic alphabet, if A is Alpha and Z is Zulu what is W?

12 Who played Chief Inspector Barlow in the television series *Softly, Softly*?

13 In which country is the state Hermitage museum?

14 Which British actor won an Oscar for the 1990 film *Reversal of Fortune*?

15 What is the capital of Spain?

16 In the animal kingdom, do scorpions lay eggs or have live young?

17 What was the nationality by birth of Lady Nancy Astor, the first woman to take her seat in the House of Commons?

18 In the animal kingdom, 'audacious jumper' and 'black widow' are both types of which creature?

19 In the proverb, what shouldn't one throw out with the bathwater?

20 What is the first name of Pasteur, the discoverer of the anthrax vaccine?

Previous Total

1,000

800

600

450

300

200

100

50

20

0

Banked

Total

Answers

1 Gardening	**11** Whisky
2 Two	**12** Stratford Johns
3 Rembrandt	**13** Russia
4 Round the neck (accept at the throat)	**14** Jeremy Irons
5 Mathematics (accept trigonometry)	**15** Madrid
	16 Live young
6 Antonio Gaudí	**17** American
7 Copper	**18** Spider (accept arachnid)
8 Celine Dion	
9 [Alfred] Hitchcock	**19** The baby
10 Bear	**20** Louis

Round 118

1 Which two molluscs are mentioned in the traditional song 'Molly Malone'?

2 Harare is the capital city of which African country?

3 In men's cricket, who won the last test match of the summer 2000 series between England and the West Indies?

4 In politics, which part of the American Congress has more members, the Senate or the House of Representatives?

5 In the human body, is the *latissimus dorsi* muscle in the back or in the leg?

6 In which decade were windscreen car tax discs introduced in the UK?

7 In education, which city's former polytechnic is now known as the John Moores University?

8 In nature, 'hart's tongue' is a type of which plant?

9 In which city might you visit Dam Square and the Anne Frank House?

10 In DIY, flock and anaglypta are both types of what?

11 In rocket science, what is known as 'lox'?

12 Who played Captain John H. Miller in the 1998 film *Saving Private Ryan*?

13 Does a spider have more or fewer legs than a fly?

14 Who starred as the live-at-home librarian in the television sitcom *Sorry!*?

15 Complete the title of this Shakespeare play, *Titus . . .* what?

16 Which English football trophy is contested annually between the winners of the Premiership and the FA Cup?

17 On the internet, for what does FTP stand?

18 Since April 2000, the UK telephone codes 020 7 and 020 8 are the new codes for which city?

19 Which fish shares its name with the type of snake that killed Cleopatra?

20 In which 1970s television sitcom was Mainwaring's catchphrase 'Stupid boy!'?

Previous Total

1,000

800

600

450

300

200

100

50

20

0

Banked

Total

Answers

1 Cockles and mussels
2 Zimbabwe (*do not* accept Rhodesia)
3 England
4 House of Representatives
5 Back
6 1920s (1921)
7 Liverpool
8 Fern
9 Amsterdam
10 Wallpaper (accept wall covering)
11 Liquid oxygen
12 Tom Hanks
13 More (a spider has 8, a fly only 6)
14 Ronnie Corbett
15 *Andronicus*
16 Charity Shield
17 File transfer protocol
18 London
19 Asp
20 *Dad's Army*

Round 119

1 Of which country is Budapest the capital city?

2 In the nursery rhyme that starts 'Hey diddle diddle', which animal jumped over the moon?

3 Which Tim Rice and Andrew Lloyd Webber stage production ran from 1972 until 1980, making it the longest-running West End musical at the time?

4 In Colorado, Larimer Square is a feature of which 'Mile High City'?

5 Is a study of fauna a study of plant life or animal life?

6 Is it true that in the human body only females have Eustachian tubes?

7 Which US city shares its name with a mythical bird that rose from its own ashes?

8 The song 'You'll Never Walk Alone' comes from which musical?

9 In law, what *F* is the American name for a serious crime?

10 In literature, did Byron write a poetic drama called *Cain* or *Abel* in 1821?

11 On which European island might one visit the Caves of Drach and Formentor?

12 Midge Ure was lead singer of which synthesiser pop band?

13 Who was the first host of the television series *The Generation Game*?

14 According to the popular song, which member of the thrush family 'Sang in Berkeley Square'?

15 What does *'al dente'* mean in Italian cooking?

16 What name is given to the slender barges specially designed for British canals so that two of them can pass each other?

17 Since World War II, who is the only leader of the Conservative Party not to have become prime minister?

18 Is your *Flexor digitorum profundus* a muscle in your arm or your chest?

19 Which French fashion designer liberated the corset as outerwear in the 1980s?

20 Which bird shares its name with the author of *Gulliver's Travels*?

Previous Total

1,000

800

600

450

300

200

100

50

20

0

Banked

Total

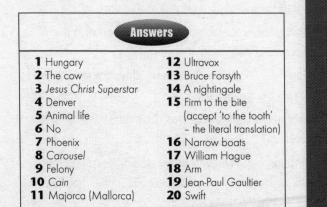

Answers

1 Hungary	**12** Ultravox
2 The cow	**13** Bruce Forsyth
3 *Jesus Christ Superstar*	**14** A nightingale
4 Denver	**15** Firm to the bite
5 Animal life	(accept 'to the tooth'
6 No	– the literal translation)
7 Phoenix	**16** Narrow boats
8 *Carousel*	**17** William Hague
9 Felony	**18** Arm
10 *Cain*	**19** Jean-Paul Gaultier
11 Majorca (Mallorca)	**20** Swift

Round 120

1 Which actress starred opposite Tom Hanks in the 1998 film *You've Got Mail*?

2 Which female sports presenter represented Wales as a gymnast?

3 Which German composer and pianist, born in 1770, became deaf but still continued to compose music?

4 Famous sons of which British city include William Gladstone and Paul McCartney?

5 Which dinosaur, with a sickle-shaped claw on each foot, has a name which comes from the Latin for 'fast plunderer'?

6 Who directed the 1962 film *Lawrence of Arabia*?

7 What is the capital of Denmark?

8 In publishing, for what do the letters *OED* stand?

9 In which century was the novelist and playwright Samuel Beckett born?

10 What twelve-year-old soprano performed at Prince Charles's 50th birthday?

11 Except in a leap year, how many days are there in the first two months of the year?

12 What musical instrument was Louis Armstrong famous for playing?

13 In fashion, which French designer did Yves St Laurent work under before opening his own couture house in Paris in 1962?

14 In which north-east England county is the Souter lighthouse?

15 In history, in what decade of the twentieth century did the Russo-Japanese War begin?

16 Which of the world's capital cities would you find on the river Tiber?

17 What is the American equivalent of the UK postcode?

18 What are the surnames of television comedy duo Mel and Griff?

19 Currently, in Britain, is Father's Day on the second or third Sunday in June?

20 Which stand-up comic and author wrote the novel *Inconceivable*?

Previous Total

1,000

800

600

450

300

200

100

50

20

0

Banked

Total

Answers

1 Meg Ryan
2 Gabby Yorath
3 Beethoven
4 Liverpool
5 Velociraptor
6 David Lean (accept Sir David Lean)
7 Copenhagen
8 *Oxford English Dictionary*
9 Twentieth century (1906)
10 Charlotte Church
11 59 days
12 Trumpet
13 Christian Dior
14 Tyne and Wear
15 The first decade (in 1904) (accept 1900s)
16 Rome
17 Zip code
18 Smith and Jones (accept Smith and Rhys Jones; do not accept just Rhys)
19 Third
20 Ben Elton

Round 121

1 In astronomy, what are the 'Andromeda Spiral' and the 'Large Cloud of Magellan'?

2 On which of Florida's famous keys might you visit Ernest Hemingway's house?

3 Which F is a single flower or branch in the head of a cauliflower?

4 Which actress played the character Molly in the 1990 film *Ghost*?

5 In the opening sequence of the television series *Porridge*, to what period of imprisonment is Fletcher sentenced?

6 In the 1981 University Boat Race, what was significant about the presence of Susan Brown in the winning boat?

7 In theatre, how many people deliver a soliloquy?

8 In pop music, which former Beatle started a film production company called Handmade Films?

9 The resorts of Sorrento and Amalfi lie close to which major Italian city?

10 In pop music, which Spice Girl sang with Dane Bowers on her single 'Out of Your Mind'?

11 Which European city's professional football team are known as 'The Grasshoppers'?

12 In the animal kingdom, 'simba' is the Swahili name for which wild creature?

13 In the American television show *Frasier*, what is the name of the dog?

14 In music, in which decade was tenor Luciano Pavarotti born?

15 In sport, which football manager is associated with the phrase 'Do I not like that!'?

16 Which fashion designer, who opened his first shop in 1970, was knighted in 2000?

17 In the 1960s, which playwright was murdered by his partner, Kenneth Halliwell?

18 The wine 'Bull's Blood' comes from which country?

19 Which 1978 Alan Parker film revolved around a drug smuggler's ordeal in a Turkish jail?

20 The Christian festival of Candlemas takes place in which month?

Previous Total

1,000

800

600

450

300

200

100

50

20

0

Banked

Total

Answers

1 Galaxies
2 Key West
3 Floret
4 Demi Moore
5 Five years
6 First woman cox
7 One
8 George Harrison
9 Naples
10 Posh Spice (accept Victoria Beckham/ Victoria Adams)

11 Zurich
12 Lion
13 Eddie
14 1930s (1935)
15 Graham Taylor
16 Paul Smith
17 Joe Orton
18 Hungary
19 *Midnight Express*
20 February

Round 122

1 In film, what is the title of the sequel to *I Know What You Did Last Summer*?

2 Which member of the royal family is chancellor of Cambridge University?

3 In literature, Ada, Richard, Esther and Lady Dedlock are characters in which Charles Dickens novel?

4 What does the organisation Gideons International traditionally leave in hotel rooms?

5 From which country did the composer and pianist Chopin come?

6 In which subject was Margaret Thatcher's first degree?

7 In pop music, are there actually seven members in the group S Club 7?

8 In sport, the West Indies won the first ever Cricket World Cup in which decade, the 1960s, the 1970s or the 1980s?

9 Did Charles Lindbergh achieve the first solo flight across the Atlantic Ocean in the year 1917 or 1927?

10 In chemistry, which element has the chemical symbol Zn?

11 In the animal kingdom, from which continent does the wombat come?

12 What is the current UK telephone dialling code for Sheffield?

13 On a Rugby Union pitch, what is the maximum distance in metres between one goal and the other?

14 In the human body, which is the largest joint?

15 Sousse and Hammamet are resorts in which north African country?

16 Complete the title of this James Bond film, *The Living . . .* what?

17 In Britain, in which year was colour television first broadcast?

18 George Fox was the founder of which religious movement?

19 Which US state is nicknamed 'the beaver state'?

20 Which actress provided the glamour in the Bob Hope and Bing Crosby *Road to* series of films?

Previous Total

1,000

800

600

450

300

200

100

50

20

0

Banked

Total

Answers

1 *I Still Know What You Did Last Summer*
2 Prince Philip (accept [HRH] the Duke of Edinburgh)
3 *Bleak House*
4 Bibles (accept New Testaments)
5 Poland
6 Chemistry (1947, Oxford)
7 Yes
8 1970s (1975)
9 1927
10 Zinc
11 Australia
12 0114
13 100 metres
14 Knee
15 [Republic of] Tunisia
16 *Daylights*
17 1967
18 Quakers (accept Society of Friends)
19 Oregon
20 Dorothy Lamour

Round 123

1 Which Radio 4 programme's signature tune is called 'Barwick Green'?

2 In 1986, Cory Aquino succeeded Ferdinand Marcos as president of which country?

3 Were the 1968 Olympics held in Mexico or Munich?

4 In jewellery, a signet and Channel-set are both types of what?

5 In which decade did the first domestic microwave oven become available in the USA?

6 Which country regained political control over Hong Kong from Britain in 1997?

7 In the human body, incisors, canines and pre-molars are all types of what?

8 Who sang 'I Just Called to Say I Love You' on the soundtrack of the 1984 film *The Woman in Red*?

9 In literature, what is the name of the 1967 book by Gabriel García Márquez about six generations of one family?

10 The island of Rhodes lies nearest to the mainland of which country?

11 In which capital city might you visit Ford's Theater and the Lincoln Memorial?

12 Complete the title of this Tom Stoppard play, *Rosencrantz and Guildenstern Are . . .* what?

13 In clothing, which M is a flat square cap worn on formal occassions by academics?

14 In music, which duo released an album called *The Sounds of Silence*, in 1966?

15 Is the Great Pyramid in Egypt taller than the Eiffel Tower?

16 Air, water, fire and what else are the four classical elements?

17 In the animal kingdom, are 'banjo', 'glass' and 'upside-down' all types of catfish or dogfish?

18 According to the proverb, what is the sincerest form of flattery?

19 What D is the unit of measurement used to describe the loudness of sound?

20 Who was the first woman to sit in the British House of Commons?

Previous Total

1,000
800
600
450
300
200
100
50
20
0

Banked

Total

Answers

1 *The Archers*
2 The Philippines
3 Mexico
4 Rings
5 1950s (1956)
6 China
7 Tooth/teeth
8 Stevie Wonder
9 *One Hundred Years of Solitude* (accept *Cien Años de Soledad*)
10 Turkey
11 Washington, DC
12 *Dead*
13 Mortarboard
14 [Paul] Simon and [Art] Garfunkel
15 No
16 Earth
17 Catfish
18 Imitation
19 Decibels
20 Lady Astor (accept Viscountess or Lady Nancy Astor)

Round 124

1 In astronomy, do 'parsecs' and 'light years' measure distance or time?

2 The dinosaurs belonged to which class of animal?

3 Former Liberal Party leader Paddy Ashdown was at one time a commander in which branch of the Royal Marines?

4 In the 1997 film *Face Off*, John Travolta co-starred with which actor?

5 In pop music, which band won both Best British Group and Best British Album at the 2000 Brit Awards?

6 In sport, which footballing knight was dubbed 'the Wizard of Dribble' by journalist Frank Butler?

7 In the animal kingdom, what does an oviparous animal do?

8 In history, in which month of 1945 did World War II end in Europe?

9 In food, in which US city did the Waldorf salad originate?

10 In sport, which Australian, in 1980, was the first mother since 1914 to win the Wimbledon singles title?

11 On a UK road sign, what is indicated by a diagonal black line on a circular white background?

12 Which UK politician's memoirs are entitled *Life in the Jungle*?

13 Haile Selassie was the emperor of which country from 1930 to 1974?

14 Which British prime minister of the 1970s had three yachts, all called *Morning Cloud*?

15 Which series of films featured the demonic child – later an adult – called Damien?

16 According to tradition, what in addition to something old, something borrowed and something new should a bride have?

17 Which English actress played Gloria in the 1996 film *Brassed Off*?

18 In food, what C is a name used for a roast of lamb or pork where the ribs are partially scraped and bent into an upright circle?

19 In the animal kingdom, 'hooded', 'striped' and 'hog-nosed' are all varieties of what?

20 In television, actor Basil Rathbone was famed for playing which Arthur Conan Doyle character on screen?

Previous Total

1,000

800

600

450

300

200

100

50

20

0

Banked

Total

Answers

1 Distance	**11** National speed limit applies
2 Reptile	**12** Michael Heseltine
3 Special Boat Service	**13** Ethiopia
4 Nicolas Cage	**14** Sir Edward Heath (accept Ted Heath)
5 Travis	**15** [The] Omen
6 [Sir] Stanley Matthews	**16** Something blue
7 Lay eggs	**17** Tara Fitzgerald
8 May (8 May 1945)	**18** Crown roast
9 New York	**19** Skunk
10 Evonne [Goolagong] Cawley	**20** [Sherlock] Holmes

Round 125

1 In music, which electronic organ was invented in the USA in 1934?

2 Is the fabric 'astrakhan' derived from sheep or llamas?

3 Complete the title of this 1993 Jilly Cooper novel, *The Man Who Made Husbands . . .* what?

4 In the animal kingdom, is it true that rabbits have two pairs of upper incisor teeth?

5 In politics, who wrote the books *The Downing Street Years* in 1993 and *The Path to Power* in 1995?

6 In the animal kingdom, did the muntjac deer originate in South America or Asia?

7 According to the proverb, a jack of all trades is master of what?

8 The scientific word for 'atom' is derived from which language, Greek or Latin?

9 In which city are the headquarters of the World Health Organization?

10 In which city in Australia is the famous opera house which sits on the water's edge?

11 In science, is the chemical element plutonium represented by the symbol Pl, Pu or Pm?

12 Name the celebrity daughter of former television presenter Johnny Ball.

13 In sport, females competed in the Olympics for the first time in which year?

14 In science, what is the first name of Fleming, who first recognised the anti-bacterial properties of the penicillin mould?

15 In what year did South Africa hold its first democratic, non-racial elections?

16 In fashion, 'Shantung silk' is named after a province of which country?

17 Kiev is the capital of which Eastern European republic?

18 In the animal kingdom, on which part of a horse is the fetlock?

19 In 1936, Jesse Owens was the star of the Olympic Games held in which city?

20 Which American band leader went missing when his plane disappeared over the English Channel during the Second World War?

Previous Total

1,000
800
600
450
300
200
100
50
20
0

Banked

Total

Answers

1 Hammond organ
2 Sheep
3 *Jealous*
4 Yes
5 Margaret Thatcher (accept Lady/Baroness Thatcher of Kestevan)
6 Asia
7 None
8 Greek
9 Geneva
10 Sydney
11 Pu
12 Zoë Ball
13 1900
14 Alexander
15 1994
16 China
17 Ukraine
18 [Lower] leg (accept also above the hoof)
19 Berlin
20 Glenn Miller

Final

Player 1

1 Which American author wrote the novel *Naked Lunch*, published in 1959?

2 Which Australian supermodel and actress is referred to as 'The Body'?

3 Which American state is known as 'the potato state'?

4 In which decade was David Frost knighted in the New Year's Honours List?

5 In the UK, St George's Hospital Medical School is part of which university?

6 What is the usual French translation for the English word 'day'?

7 Harrison Ford played Dr Richard Kimble in which 1993 film?

8 In history, was the first widespread use of trench warfare during World War I or the American Civil War?

9 In nature, two species of ambrosia beetle have been responsible for the widespread destruction of which tree?

10 What B is a group of islands in the Atlantic Ocean that gained independence within the Commonwealth in 1973?

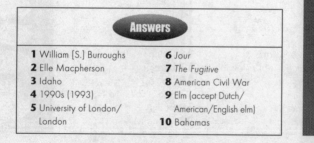

Answers

1 William [S.] Burroughs
2 Elle Macpherson
3 Idaho
4 1990s (1993)
5 University of London/ London

6 Jour
7 The Fugitive
8 American Civil War
9 Elm (accept Dutch/ American/English elm)
10 Bahamas

Final

Player 2

1 Four and twenty of what type of bird were baked in a pie, according to the rhyme?

2 In which Monty Python film does Graham Chapman play King Arthur and God?

3 The English admiral and explorer Sir Francis Drake was born in which century: the sixteenth or seventeenth?

4 In the animal kingdom, what *P* is another name for the cougar or mountain lion?

5 In which German city is the largest Gothic cathedral in Northern Europe?

6 In transport, what *B* is a small post marking a traffic island?

7 In which capital city might you visit the FBI building and the White House?

8 Which noted English dramatist and composer penned the song line 'Don't put your daughter on the stage, Mrs Worthington'?

9 In the animal kingdom, is a tench a fish or a frog?

10 John Wesley was the founder of which worldwide religious movement?

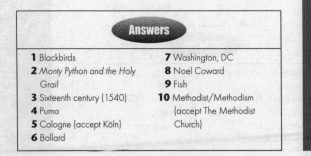

Answers

1 Blackbirds
2 *Monty Python and the Holy Grail*
3 Sixteenth century (1540)
4 Puma
5 Cologne (accept Köln)
6 Bollard
7 Washington, DC
8 Noel Coward
9 Fish
10 Methodist/Methodism (accept The Methodist Church)

Final

Player 1

1 What name is given to a first-year student at an American university?

2 Which television comic performs the characters Tim Nice But Dim and Tory Boy?

3 Does a comet's tail always point away from or towards the sun?

4 Which American rock singer and guitarist played with The E Street Band?

5 Introduced in the mid-1950s, what sort of musical instrument is a Fender Stratocaster?

6 How fast must an object travel to escape the Earth's gravity: 20,000 or 40,000 kilometres per hour?

7 In religion, what C is an ankle-length garment often worn by clergymen?

8 Which Republican did JFK defeat in the 1960 American presidential election?

9 In architecture, what A is the name given to an arched or domed recess at the east end of a church?

10 Which castle is home to the Earls of Groan in Mervyn Peake's novels?

Answers

1 Freshman (accept 'fresher' or 'frosh')
2 Harry Enfield
3 Away
4 Bruce Springsteen
5 [Electric] guitar
6 40,000 kilometres per hour
7 Cassock
8 Richard Nixon
9 Apse
10 Gormenghast

Final

Player 2

1 In history, in which 1848 text did Karl Marx write that the 'spectre of Communism' was 'haunting Europe'?

2 The term for which extinct reptiles comes from the Greek for 'terrible lizard'?

3 In geography, in which US state would you find Tulsa?

4 The IBF, WFO and WBC are governing bodies in which sport?

5 What artistic movement was headed by André Breton in the 1920s and followed on from Dadaism?

6 In humans, in what part of the body would you find the talus?

7 In computer technology, for what do the initials AI stand?

8 In darts, how many points would you score if you hit eighteen, double fifteen and seven?

9 In television, which US sitcom created spin-offs *Mork and Mindy* and *Laverne and Shirley*?

10 As a result of a sixteenth-century law, what colour must all Venetian gondolas be painted?

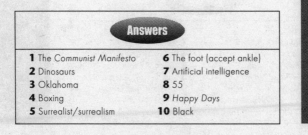

Answers

1 The *Communist Manifesto*	**6** The foot (accept ankle)
2 Dinosaurs	**7** Artificial intelligence
3 Oklahoma	**8** 55
4 Boxing	**9** *Happy Days*
5 Surrealist/surrealism	**10** Black

Final

Player 1

1 In politics, what name is given to the elected head of state of a republic?

2 What 1994 animated film features a lion cub called Simba?

3 In history, which palace in Edinburgh was the scene of the murder of David Rizzio, the alleged lover of Mary Queen of Scots?

4 In television, what do the initials in the name of the television channel CNN stand for?

5 Who became president of South Africa on 10 May 1994?

6 What *T* is an area in the northern hemisphere characterised by the absence of trees?

7 In the Christian calendar, is Ash Wednesday the first or the last day of Lent?

8 In what 1982 film does Richard Gere star as a naval officer who falls in love with Debra Winger?

9 In football, name the Arsenal manager who worked in Japan before coming to England?

10 In medicine, how many types of penicillin are there, two or four?

Answers

1 President	**6** Tundra
2 *The Lion King*	**7** The first
3 Palace of Holyrood House (accept Holyrood)	**8** *An Officer and a Gentleman*
4 Cable News Network	**9** Arsene Wenger
5 Nelson Mandela (accept Nelson Rolihlahla Mandela)	**10** Four (Penicillin-G types, ampicillin, penicillinase-resistants and antiseudomonal)

Final

Player 2

1 In transport, when were pelican crossings introduced to Britain, 1958 or 1968?

2 In which English city would you find King's College Chapel, famous for its annual broadcast service?

3 Which country is larger in terms of area and population, France or Spain?

4 In snooker, if you potted the following balls in the correct order, how many points would you score: two reds and two blacks?

5 In music, which note comes before doh on the doh, ray, me scale?

6 In language, what A is the term for the denial of the existence of any God or gods?

7 In the television series, did Tyne Daley play Cagney or Lacey?

8 In architecture, what A is the name given to a recess in the wall of a room?

9 Which noted Spanish poet and playwright was shot without trial in the Spanish Civil War in 1936?

10 In which year were disposable plastic razors marketed – 1964 or 1974?

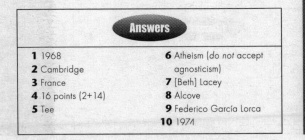

Answers

1 1968
2 Cambridge
3 France
4 16 points (2+14)
5 Tee

6 Atheism (do not accept agnosticism)
7 [Beth] Lacey
8 Alcove
9 Federico García Lorca
10 1974

Final

Player 1

1 In literature, name the 1961 Muriel Spark novel about an Edinburgh schoolmistress and her group of favoured pupils.

2 Divide the number of degrees in a circle by the number of sides of a square.

3 Which noted eighteenth-century figure said: 'When a man is tired of London, he is tired of life'?

4 Which 1980s British television sitcom was set at Maplins holiday camp?

5 Which long-running television show has been presented by Eamonn Andrews and Michael Aspel?

6 An 'eland' is what type of animal, from Africa?

7 In mythology, Osiris was the ruler of the underworld for which ancient civilisation?

8 In 1927, the FA Cup was won by a non-English club for the first time. Who were the winners?

9 In medicine, when measuring blood pressure, is the 'diastolic pressure' the higher or lower of the two figures?

10 What were the surnames of the English comic duo Pete 'n' Dud?

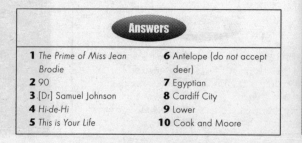

Answers

1 *The Prime of Miss Jean Brodie*
2 90
3 [Dr] Samuel Johnson
4 *Hi-de-Hi*
5 *This is Your Life*
6 Antelope (do not accept deer)
7 Egyptian
8 Cardiff City
9 Lower
10 Cook and Moore

Final

Player 2

1 In World Wars I and II, what kind of German vessel was a U-boat?

2 In football, which country did Diego Maradona captain during the World Cup finals of 1986 and 1990?

3 Is the town of Wallsend at the east or west end of Hadrian's Wall?

4 In religion, what is the term given to the appearance of wounds or scars corresponding to those of the crucified Christ on a human's body?

5 In 1974, an unsuccessful kidnap attempt was made in London on which member of the British royal family?

6 In mathematics, the sides of a tetrahedron are what shape?

7 Who directed the 1960 film *Psycho*?

8 In which US state is Daytona Beach?

9 Which nineteenth-century English poet wrote an epitaph for the grave of his Newfoundland dog, Bosun, at Newstead Abbey?

10 Which band's 1977 album *Rumours* became one of the biggest-selling albums of all time?

Answers

1 Submarine	**6** Triangular/triangles
2 Argentina	**7** Sir Alfred Hitchcock
3 East	(accept Hitchcock)
4 Stigmata	**8** Florida
5 Princess Anne (accept	**9** Lord Byron
Princess Royal)	**10** Fleetwood Mac

Final

Player 1

1 In which Shakespeare play does the leading man say, 'Age cannot wither her, nor custom stale her infinite variety' – *Antony and Cleopatra* or *Hamlet*?

2 Who was Oliver Hardy's comedy partner?

3 Which British World War II leader was born at Blenheim Palace?

4 What type of common British snake will play dead in order to deter predators – the grass snake or the adder?

5 According to the nursery rhyme, who met a pieman going to the fair?

6 In the animal kingdom, do electric eels actually produce electricity?

7 In geography, which Central American country lies between Nicaragua and Panama?

8 In music, did the Beatles receive their MBEs in the 1960s or the 1970s?

9 What B is a name used for a puffed-up, backcombed hairstyle, worn by both men and women?

10 Vespa and Lambretta are famous manufacturers of what type of vehicle?

Answers

1 *Antony and Cleopatra*	**6** Yes
2 Stan Laurel	**7** Costa Rica
3 [Sir] Winston Churchill	**8** 1960s (1965)
4 Grass snake	**9** Bouffant
5 Simple Simon	**10** Scooters (mopeds)

Final

Player 2

1 In science, what *B* are tiny organisms, ranging in length from 1 to 10 micrometers?

2 What type of animal is an 'addax' – an antelope, a horse or a goat?

3 Which Hollywood actress starred in the 1933 film *She Done Him Wrong* based on a play written by her?

4 In politics, what *V* is the name given to an expression of opinion by ballot?

5 Name the Sydney Olympic champion who asked in 1996 to be shot if he went near a boat again.

6 In classical music, which composer was born in Salzburg and composed *Don Giovanni* in 1787?

7 In travel, which Scandinavian country is famous for its fjords?

8 Which *M* was the arch-enemy of Doctor Who?

9 In literature, complete the title of the 1924 children's classic by A. A. Milne: *When We Were Very . . .* what?

10 In maths, what is 63 divided by 7?

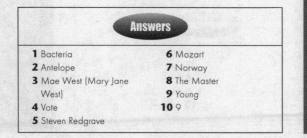

Answers

1 Bacteria
2 Antelope
3 Mae West (Mary Jane West)
4 Vote
5 Steven Redgrave

6 Mozart
7 Norway
8 The Master
9 Young
10 9

Player 1

1 Under what pseudonym did children's author George Remi write the Tintin books?

2 There were two 'opium wars'. The first was between China and Britain, the second between Britain and which other country against China?

3 Are birds of prey carnivores or herbivores?

4 The stately home Harewood House is in which English county?

5 In meteorology, what S was a phenomenon known as 'London Particular' when it was first recognised?

6 In geography, which European capital is home to the ancient Acropolis?

7 Which D. H. Lawrence novel of 1913 tells the story of Paul Morel and his destructive relationship with his mother?

8 In chinaware, which word normally precedes Crown Derby, Doulton and Worcester?

9 Which popular American singer starred in and directed the 1965 film None But the Brave?

10 In nature, can the cormorant or the heron swim deeper?

Answers

1 Hergé	6 Athens
2 France	7 Sons and Lovers
3 Carnivores	8 Royal
4 Yorkshire (accept West Yorkshire)	9 Frank Sinatra
5 Smog	10 Cormorant

Player 2

1 In food, what *B* is a type of toffee made using butter?

2 Traditionally, is Ikebana the Japanese or Chinese art of flower arranging?

3 What *S* is a cone of calcite rock rising up from the floor of a limestone cavern?

4 Which British actor played Lee Harvey Oswald in the 1991 film *JFK*?

5 What *A* is the name given to the absence of the sense of pain?

6 In geography, Beverly Hills is situated within which American city?

7 In science, centigrade is the former name of what temperature scale?

8 What is the traditional Chinese medical technique in which metal needles are inserted into the skin?

9 In UK politics, is the Home Office currently situated in Downing Street or Queen Anne's Gate?

10 Which British author wrote the novels *The End of the Affair*, *The Heart of the Matter* and *The Quiet American*?

Answers

1 Butterscotch	**6** Los Angeles
2 Japanese	**7** Celsius
3 Stalagmite	**8** Acupuncture
4 Gary Oldman	**9** Queen Anne's Gate
5 Analgesia (accept analgesic)	**10** Graham Greene

Final

Player 1

1 In religion, in the Judeo-Christian tradition what C is the name given to the admission of sin?

2 In which English county is Stansted Airport?

3 In maths, an acute angle is an angle between zero and how many degrees?

4 In the animal kingdom, what *I* is a large lizard with a spiny crest along its back?

5 Which Jamaican reggae singer's albums included *Exodus* and *Natty Dread*?

6 Which Italian city has been nicknamed 'the Jewel of the Adriatic' and 'the Bride of the Sea'?

7 In golf, who has competed with the USA in the Ryder Cup since 1979: Great Britain or Europe?

8 James Nisbet's series of children's books from 1949 featured which brother and sister?

9 In which decade of the twentieth century did the Supreme Court of the United States declare racial segregation in schools illegal?

10 In which English town was William Shakespeare born?

Answers

1 Confession (accept Chapter of Faults)
2 Essex
3 90 degrees
4 Iguana
5 Bob Marley (accept Robert Nesta Marley)
6 Venice
7 Europe
8 Janet and John
9 1950s (1954)
10 Stratford-upon-Avon

Final

Player 2

1 Which bigoted cockney pensioner was created by writer Johnny Speight?

2 In nature, what is a male fox called?

3 In which religion would a 'mezuzah' be attached to the doorpost of the house as a sign of faith?

4 Complete the title of this James Bond film, *The Spy Who* . . .

5 In medicine, are amino acids the building blocks of proteins or vitamins?

6 In television, which Dame stars with Geoffrey Palmer in the romantic sitcom *As Time Goes By*?

7 Where does the statue called 'Eros' stand in London?

8 In mammals, what C are the teeth found between the incisors and pre-molars?

9 What was the name given to unlicensed radio stations such as Radio London and Radio Caroline?

10 In classical music, what is the lowest-pitched instrument of the violin family?

Answers

1 Alf Garnett	**6** Judi Dench
2 A dog fox (accept dog)	**7** Piccadilly Circus
3 Jewish (Judaism)	**8** Canine
4 Loved Me	**9** Pirate radio
5 Proteins	**10** The double bass

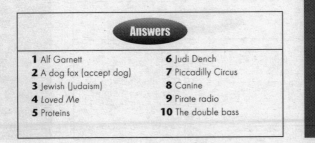

Player 1

1 Where is John Nash's domed Royal Pavilion?

2 Which boy band took their name from the postcode of their native Walthamstow?

3 What C is a crushed grain product often served steamed with North African dishes?

4 In the game of chess, how many squares can a king move at any one time?

5 What C is the name given to a regulation requiring a person to be indoors by a certain hour of the night?

6 In the animal kingdom, by what name is the species *Felis catus* commonly known?

7 Which brave teenager went to school at Sunnydale High in an American TV series which shares her name?

8 Was Ludwig Wittgenstein a philosopher, artist or composer?

9 In UK politics, who announced in June 1991 that she would not be standing for re-election as MP for Finchley?

10 The city of Montgomery is the capital of which US state, situated on the Gulf of Mexico?

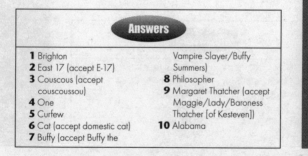

Answers

1 Brighton

2 East 17 (accept E-17)

3 Couscous (accept couscoussou)

4 One

5 Curfew

6 Cat (accept domestic cat)

7 Buffy (accept Buffy the Vampire Slayer/Buffy Summers)

8 Philosopher

9 Margaret Thatcher (accept Maggie/Lady/Baroness Thatcher [of Kesteven])

10 Alabama

Final

Player 2

1 The modern rules of which sport were named after the Eighth Marquess of Queensberry in 1867?

2 In the human body how many pairs of ribs are there?

3 In which country is the beach resort 'Surfer's Paradise' found?

4 Which 1961 Disney animated film features the characters Pongo and Perdita?

5 Which is Scotland's oldest university?

6 What type of bird eats the eggs and young of other birds and is thought to bring bad luck?

7 In English law, what does a coroner investigate as the main part of his job?

8 In TV, which comedy character was noted for his bad cooking, poor personal hygiene and never-ending supply of 'cunning plans'?

9 What, according to the Greek mathematician Euclid, is the shortest distance between two points?

10 In theatre, was the first complete edition of Shakespeare's plays called the 'First Folio' or the 'First Quarto'?

Answers

1 Boxing	**7** Death (cause of death/ sudden or suspicious death)
2 Twelve	
3 Australia	
4 *101 Dalmations*	**8** Baldrick
5 St Andrews	**9** Straight line
6 Magpie	**10** First Folio (accept Folio)

Final

Player 1

1 In pop music, during the 1970s who used the persona Ziggy Stardust?

2 What nationality is the heart transplant pioneer Christiaan Barnard?

3 In which decade were tea bags first sold for domestic consumption in the UK?

4 In which decade did the BBC TV programme *Holiday* begin?

5 Is a 'French pleat' a hairstyle or a way of tying a tie?

6 In what year did the Sex Pistols make their infamous appearance on Bill Grundy's show, *Thames Today* – 1973 or 1976?

7 Which female black spider usually has a red hourglass marking on her underside?

8 What life-saving device did American Benjamin Franklin invent in 1753?

9 The US black leader Malcolm X was born in which decade: 1920s or 1930s?

10 Which city in the United States is the home of the Library of Congress?

Answers

1 David Bowie
2 South African
3 1950s (1952)
4 1960s
5 Hairstyle
6 1976

7 Black widow (spider)/ red-back spider
8 Lightning conductor (accept lightning rod)
9 1920s (1925)
10 Washington, DC

Final

Player 2

1 In mythology, which stone weapon is most commonly associated with the Nordic god Thor – a hammer or an axe?

2 Who is the patron saint of tax collectors?

3 Which soap actor had hits with the songs 'Every Loser Wins' and 'Heartbeat'?

4 In food, from which animal does pancetta originate?

5 Which male actor played Ned Land in the 1954 film *20,000 Leagues Under the Sea*?

6 Which twentieth-century British monarch said: 'We have our part to play in restoring the shattered fabric of civilisation'?

7 In British politics, which institution was given the power to set interest rates in 1997?

8 Cross-country skiing and which other sport make up the biathlon in the Winter Olympics?

9 For what are the caves at Lascaux in France most famous?

10 What is the capital of Hungary?

Answers

1 Hammer
2 Saint Matthew (accept Levi)
3 Nick Berry
4 Pig
5 Kirk Douglas
6 George VI (said in his VJ Day speech)
7 The Bank of England
8 Rifle shooting
9 Ancient cave paintings (accept cave drawings/engravings/animal paintings)
10 Budapest

Final

Player 1

1 Whose operas include *Lohengrin* and *The Flying Dutchman*?

2 What is the name given to a machine which transforms mechanical energy into electrical energy?

3 Which book of the Bible is set in Persia – Esther or Ruth?

4 In UK military terms, what is a 'wren'?

5 In which 1964 film did Michael Caine play Lieutenant Gonville Bromhead?

6 Malcolm Campbell set a new world land speed record in 1935. What was the name of the vehicle?

7 In food, is 'roti' a general Indian term for bread or meat?

8 What is the official language of Tunisia?

9 The Turkish flag is made up of two symbols – a moon and what?

10 Who wrote the classic book *The Compleat Angler*?

Answers

1 Wagner (Richard Wilhelm Wagner)
2 Dynamo
3 Esther
4 A member of the Women's Royal Naval Service (WRNS)
5 *Zulu*
6 *Bluebird*
7 Bread
8 Arabic
9 Star
10 Isaak Walton

Final

Player 2

1 In nature, what *D* is a plant traditionally considered an antidote to a nettle sting?

2 In monetary terms, what do the initials GNP represent?

3 In TV, in which 1970s US drama series did a large family run a saw mill in the mountains of Virginia?

4 'Black' and 'Bewick's' are types of which bird?

5 Which Asian capital city is known by its inhabitants as 'Krung Thep'?

6 In nature, what is the opposite of diurnal?

7 In nature, the 'purple emperor' is a variety of what insect?

8 In sport, which British tennis star won his first tournament for two years in October 2000?

9 In the card game cribbage how many points are scored for a combination of cards which add up to fifteen?

10 Which Austrian composer wrote a piano quintet in 1819 known as *The Trout*?

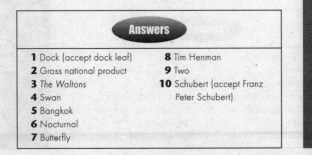

Answers

1 Dock (accept dock leaf)
2 Gross national product
3 *The Waltons*
4 Swan
5 Bangkok
6 Nocturnal
7 Butterfly
8 Tim Henman
9 Two
10 Schubert (accept Franz Peter Schubert)

Final

Player 1

1 In seventeenth-century literature, who wrote the religious story *The Pilgrim's Progress*?

2 Who, with Friedrich Engels, published the *Communist Manifesto* in 1848?

3 Which TV presenter fronted the 1960s satire show *That Was The Week That Was* and more recently *Through the Keyhole*?

4 What berries are the fruits of the blackthorn and are often soaked in gin to make Christmas liqueur?

5 In the musical team Gilbert and Sullivan, which of them wrote the words?

6 Who starred as 'the Scarlet Pimpernel' in the recent TV series?

7 In which country was the painter Marc Chagall born – Estonia or Belarus?

8 In history, who succeeded George Washington as president of the United States?

9 On the World Wide Web, which country does '.fr' represent?

10 In pop music, 'A Whiter Shade of Pale' was a number one hit in 1967 for which group?

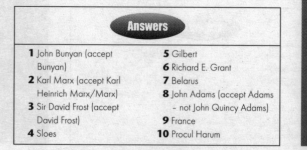

Answers

1 John Bunyan (accept Bunyan)
2 Karl Marx (accept Karl Heinrich Marx/Marx)
3 Sir David Frost (accept David Frost)
4 Sloes
5 Gilbert
6 Richard E. Grant
7 Belarus
8 John Adams (accept Adams – not John Quincy Adams)
9 France
10 Procul Harum

Final

Player 2

1 In biology, what C is the name given to the structure in a cell nucleus that carries the genes?

2 In *Peter Pan*, what was the name of Captain Hook's ship?

3 In geography, Riyadh is the royal capital of which country?

4 In history, Singapore surrendered to which country's army on 15 February 1942?

5 In nature, what *E* is a type of northern sea duck that has soft down feathers – often used for quilts?

6 In TV, name Jason Priestley's character in the US series *Beverly Hills 90210*.

7 The Central School of Speech and Drama in London is based in which former theatre?

8 Which Spanish city is the setting for Bizet's *Carmen*, de Molina's *Don Juan* and Mozart's *Marriage of Figaro*?

9 In the sport beach volleyball, how many players are there per team: two or six?

10 Which saint was the first Archbishop of Canterbury?

Answers

1 Chromosome	**7** Embassy Theatre
2 The *Jolly Roger*	**8** Seville
3 Saudi Arabia	**9** Two
4 Japan	**10** Saint Augustine (accept
5 Eider duck	Augustine)
6 Brandon Walsh (accept	
Brandon)	

Final

Player 1

1 In the Bible, what was Lot's wife turned into for disobeying God's order not to look back?

2 Which Swedish-born actress played the main female role in the 1943 film *For Whom the Bell Tolls*?

3 In human biology, what is the dark brown pigment normally found in the skin?

4 The title of Wilbur Smith's first novel was *When the Lion . . .* what?

5 Traditionally, what type of food is set off rolling down a hill in an annual event at Cooper's Hill, Gloucestershire?

6 In TV, name the actor who played George Carter in the cop series *The Sweeney*.

7 In art, in which century was the Pre-Raphaelite school of artists established?

8 Which landmark BBC building officially opened on 1 May 1932?

9 Name the British fashion designer who had a long relationship with Sex Pistols manager Malcolm McLaren between 1965 and 1981.

10 The ship *Titanic* was owned and operated by which liner company?

Answers

1 A pillar of salt
2 Ingrid Bergman
3 Melanin
4 Feeds
5 Gloucester cheese (accept cheese)
6 Dennis Waterman
7 Nineteenth century
8 Broadcasting House
9 Vivienne Westwood
10 White Star Line

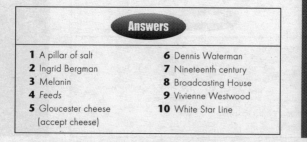

Player 2

1 In the animal kingdom, what name is given to any front-fanged venomous snake of the family *Viperidae*?

2 Which London theatre was founded by Sir Bernard Miles?

3 How old was Stevie Wonder when he began recording music – 12, 16, or 21?

4 In British history, in 1833, what was William Wilberforce instrumental in abolishing in the British Commonwealth?

5 In Greek mythology, who was the messenger of the gods?

6 In biology, what C is the smallest independent unit of life?

7 In maths, what is 20 per cent of £5?

8 What 1950s comedy radio show starred Spike Milligan, Harry Secombe, Michael Bentine and Peter Sellers?

9 In history, which Roman Caesar was stabbed by Brutus?

10 In which sport is a 44 lb granite stone pushed down a stretch of ice towards a target?

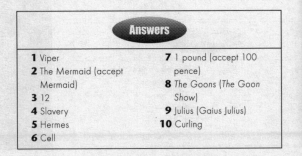

Answers

1 Viper
2 The Mermaid (accept Mermaid)
3 12
4 Slavery
5 Hermes
6 Cell
7 1 pound (accept 100 pence)
8 *The Goons* (*The Goon Show*)
9 Julius (Gaius Julius)
10 Curling

Final

Player 1

1 What *B* is a device used to slow down or stop the movement of a vehicle?

2 In nature, are earthworms hermaphrodites?

3 Was Orphism an ancient Greek or an ancient Roman religion?

4 Which famous singer played a female baseball player in the film *A League of Their Own*?

5 Who was sworn in as the 36th president of the United States within hours of the assassination of JFK – Lyndon B. Johnson or Richard Nixon?

6 In pop music, what itsy-bitsy, teeny-weeny garment was worn in a song sung by Brian Hyland?

7 In literature, was Rostand's *Cyrano de Bergerac* written in the eighteenth, nineteenth or twentieth century?

8 Which American civil rights campaigner is remembered for his 'I have a dream' speech?

9 In nature, do stinging nettles or dead nettles have colourful flowers?

10 In biology, what part of the body do flying fish use to propel themselves out of the water?

Answers

1 Brake

2 Yes

3 Ancient Greek

4 Madonna

5 Lyndon B. Johnson

6 Yellow polka-dot bikini (accept bikini)

7 Nineteenth

8 Martin Luther King (Jr)

9 Dead nettles

10 Tail (accept pectoral fins)

Final

Player 2

1 In the children's stories, what was Captain Pugwash: a pirate or a soldier?

2 In geography, in which country would you find the Sierra Madre mountain system?

3 Which British actor adapted, directed and starred in the 1989 film *Henry V*?

4 In fashion, what G is a type of boneless, elastic corset?

5 In science, is cryogenics the study of very high or very low temperatures?

6 In the film *The Wizard of Oz*, how is Dorothy transported over the rainbow?

7 In politics, was Britain forced out of the ERM on 'Black Monday' or 'Black Wednesday' in 1992?

8 John Parrott and which famous footballer are team captains on the TV programme *A Question of Sport*?

9 Which P is an Italian composer who wrote the aria 'Nessun Dorma', made famous by Pavarotti at the 1990 World Cup?

10 What D is the common name for the flakes of scurf shed from the scalp?

Answers

1 Pirate

2 Mexico (accept United Mexican States)

3 Kenneth Branagh

4 Girdle

5 Low

6 By a tornado

7 Black Wednesday

8 Ally McCoist

9 [Giacomo] Puccini

10 Dandruff

Tie-breakers

1 The Area of Outstanding Natural Beauty called Dedham Vale overlaps two counties – name either.

2 In travel, is the Italian city of Florence to the north or south of Rome?

3 In the animal kingdom, what S is a small, mouse-like, insect-eating mammal with a long pointed snout?

4 In nature, are slow-worms categorised as snakes or lizards?

5 In what 1960s sitcom would you find the characters Morticia, Gomez and Wednesday?

6 Which Chinese city gave its name to a method of serving duck with pancakes, cucumber and Hoi Sin sauce?

7 The 1975 novel *Last Bus to Woodstock* was the first to feature which fictional detective?

8 In maths, what is 108 divided by 9?

9 In history, what A was a region in eastern Canada that became the site of the first permanent French colony in North America?

10 In the animal kingdom, what is the collective noun for a group of crows?

Answers

1 Essex or Suffolk

2 North

3 Shrew

4 Lizards

5 *The Addams Family*

6 Beijing (accept Peking)

7 Inspector Morse

8 12

9 Acadia (accept Acadie)

10 Murder (accept clan or hover)

Tie-breakers

1 In geography, Kuala Lumpur is the capital of what country?

2 In science, H_2O is the chemical symbol for what?

3 In which century did Louis Blériot become the first man to successfully fly an aeroplane across the English Channel?

4 In politics, which has more members: the House of Representatives in the United States, or the House of Commons in the UK?

5 The Scottish city of Glasgow stands on the banks of which river?

6 In literature, 'The Knight's', 'The Miller's' and 'The Cook's Tale' all appear in which Geoffrey Chaucer work?

7 In art, what W is a renowned Staffordshire pottery company?

8 Which Swedish-born actress played Queen Christina in the 1933 film of that name?

9 What animal did comedian Freddie Starr allegedly eat according to a 1986 *Sun* headline?

10 What B is a famous type of soft cheese that originated in a region of France to the north-east of Paris?

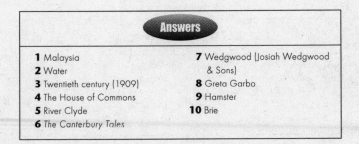

Answers

1 Malaysia
2 Water
3 Twentieth century (1909)
4 The House of Commons
5 River Clyde
6 *The Canterbury Tales*

7 Wedgwood (Josiah Wedgwood & Sons)
8 Greta Garbo
9 Hamster
10 Brie